Human Trafficking

Other Books in the Current Controversies Series

Human Trafficking

Dedria Bryfonski, Book Editor

GREENHAVEN PRESS
A part of Gale, Cengage Learning

GALE
CENGAGE Learning·

Detroit • New York • San Francisco • New Haven, Conn • Waterville, Maine • London

Elizabeth Des Chenes, *Director, Publishing Solutions*

© 2013 Greenhaven Press, a part of Gale, Cengage Learning

Gale and Greenhaven Press are registered trademarks used herein under license.

For more information, contact:
Greenhaven Press
27500 Drake Rd.
Farmington Hills, MI 48331-3535
Or you can visit our Internet site at gale.cengage.com

For product information and technology assistance, contact us at

Gale Customer Support, 1-800-877-4253
For permission to use material from this text or product, submit all requests online at www.cengage.com/permissions

Further permissions questions can be emailed to permissionrequest@cengage.com

Articles in Greenhaven Press anthologies are often edited for length to meet page requirements. In addition, original titles of these works are changed to clearly present the main thesis and to explicitly indicate the author's opinion. Every effort is made to ensure that Greenhaven Press accurately reflects the original intent of the authors. Every effort has been made to trace the owners of copyrighted material.

Cover image copyright © Rafael Ben-Ari/Alamy.

LIBRARY OF CONGRESS CATALOGING-IN-PUBLICATION DATA

Human trafficking / Dedria Bryfonski, book editor.
   p. cm. -- (Current controversies)
  Includes bibliographical references and index.
  ISBN 978-0-7377-6231-0 (hardcover) -- ISBN 978-0-7377-6232-7 (pbk.)
  1. Human trafficking. 2. Human trafficking--Prevention. I. Bryfonski, Dedria, editor of compilation.
  HQ281.H832 2013
  306.3'62--dc23

                          2013001036

Printed in the United States of America
2 3 4 5 6   17 16 15 14 13

Contents

Chapter 1: What Factors Contribute to Human Trafficking?

Chapter 2: Should Internet Sites Used for Sex Trafficking Be Shut Down?

Yes: Internet Sites Used for Sex Trafficking Should Be Shut Down

No: Internet Sites Used for Sex Trafficking Should Not Be Shut Down

Chapter 3: Does Globalization Promote Human Trafficking?

Yes: Globalization Promotes Human Trafficking

No: Globalization Does Not Promote Human Trafficking

Chapter 4: How Can Human Trafficking Be Addressed?

Foreword

By definition, controversies are "discussions of questions in which opposing opinions clash" (*Webster's Twentieth Century Dictionary Unabridged*). Few would deny that controversies are a pervasive part of the human condition and exist on virtually every level of human enterprise. Controversies transpire between individuals and among groups, within nations and between nations. Controversies supply the grist necessary for progress by providing challenges and challengers to the status quo. They also create atmospheres where strife and warfare can flourish. A world without controversies would be a peaceful world; but it also would be, by and large, static and prosaic.

The Series' Purpose

The purpose of the Current Controversies series is to explore many of the social, political, and economic controversies dominating the national and international scenes today. Titles selected for inclusion in the series are highly focused and specific. For example, from the larger category of criminal justice, Current Controversies deals with specific topics such as police brutality, gun control, white collar crime, and others. The debates in Current Controversies also are presented in a useful, timeless fashion. Articles and book excerpts included in each title are selected if they contribute valuable, long-range ideas to the overall debate. And wherever possible, current information is enhanced with historical documents and other relevant materials. Thus, while individual titles are current in focus, every effort is made to ensure that they will not become quickly outdated. Books in the Current Controversies series will remain important resources for librarians, teachers, and students for many years.

In addition to keeping the titles focused and specific, great care is taken in the editorial format of each book in the series. Book introductions and chapter prefaces are offered to provide background material for readers. Chapters are organized around several key questions that are answered with diverse opinions representing all points on the political spectrum. Materials in each chapter include opinions in which authors clearly disagree as well as alternative opinions in which authors may agree on a broader issue but disagree on the possible solutions. In this way, the content of each volume in Current Controversies mirrors the mosaic of opinions encountered in society. Readers will quickly realize that there are many viable answers to these complex issues. By questioning each author's conclusions, students and casual readers can begin to develop the critical thinking skills so important to evaluating opinionated material.

Current Controversies is also ideal for controlled research. Each anthology in the series is composed of primary sources taken from a wide gamut of informational categories including periodicals, newspapers, books, US and foreign government documents, and the publications of private and public organizations. Readers will find factual support for reports, debates, and research papers covering all areas of important issues. In addition, an annotated table of contents, an index, a book and periodical bibliography, and a list of organizations to contact are included in each book to expedite further research.

Perhaps more than ever before in history, people are confronted with diverse and contradictory information. During the Persian Gulf War, for example, the public was not only treated to minute-to-minute coverage of the war, it was also inundated with critiques of the coverage and countless analyses of the factors motivating US involvement. Being able to sort through the plethora of opinions accompanying today's major issues, and to draw one's own conclusions, can be a complicated and frustrating struggle. It is the editors' hope that Current Controversies will help readers with this struggle.

Introduction

> *"Human trafficking is global in scope, oc-*
> *curring in 161 countries. . . . It is also*
> *the fastest growing criminal activity in*
> *the world."*

When many Americans hear the term *slavery*, they think of the North Atlantic slave trade that began in 1619 and ended in 1865 with the conclusion of the Civil War. During this 246-year period, it is estimated that approximately eleven million Africans were transported across the Atlantic against their will and sold into slavery in North and South America. At the height of slavery in the United States, the national census of 1860 counted 4 million slaves. As large as these numbers are, they are eclipsed by the number of slaves in the world today, estimated by the United Nations to be between twenty-seven and thirty million. Modern-day slavery is also significantly more profitable than slavery during the earlier era. At that time, the price of a slave was approximately $40,000 in current dollars, adjusted for inflation. Today, depending on the country and circumstances, the average price of a human being is only $90, according to leading abolitionist Kevin Bales.

What is modern-day slavery? According to the CNN Freedom Project, "Slavery occurs when one person completely controls another person, using violence or the threat of violence to maintain that control; exploits them economically; pays them nothing; and they cannot walk away."

The United Nations Trafficking Protocol calls human trafficking "the recruitment, transport, transfer, harboring or receipt of a person by such means as threat or use of force or other forms of coercion, of abduction, or fraud or deception for the purpose of exploitation." The protocol includes three elements:

1. the action of trafficking, which means the recruitment, transportation, transfer, harboring, or receipt of persons;

2. the means of trafficking, which includes threat or use of force, deception, coercion, abuse of power, or position of vulnerability;

3. the purpose of trafficking, which is always exploitation.

In the words of the trafficking protocol, article 3: "Exploitation shall include, at a minimum, the exploitation of the prostitution of others or other forms of sexual exploitation, forced labor or services, slavery or practices similar to slavery, servitude or the removal of organs."

Human trafficking is global in scope, occurring in 161 countries. The United Nations Office on Drugs and Crime estimates that profits of $32 billion are generated annually from human trafficking, making it the third largest criminal activity in the world, behind illegal drugs and arms trafficking. It is also the fastest growing criminal activity in the world. Its victims are usually young, with the majority being between eighteen and twenty-four years of age. In 80% of the cases, the victim is a woman; in 50%, a child, according to Alexis A. Aronowitz in *Human Trafficking, Human Misery: The Global Trade in Human Beings*. In 54% of the cases, the recruiter is unknown to the victim; in 46% of the cases, the victim is trafficked by an acquaintance or relative.

Residents of poor countries are particularly vulnerable to human traffickers. For example, girls are lured into certain bars in Vietnam where they are put on display and then auctioned off, usually to a trafficker from China, Taiwan, or South Korea. Although the girls often think they are to be married, they end up working in sweatshops or as prostitutes.

Ivory Coast in West Africa is the world's leading producer of cocoa beans. It is also the site of some of the world's most egregious human rights abuses. Boys age twelve to sixteen, most of them from neighboring Mali, are lured by traffickers, who sell them to cocoa farmers. These boys harvest the cocoa beans under inhumane conditions.

The United States is not immune from human trafficking. According to Humantrafficking.com, approximately 17,500 foreign nationals are trafficked annually in the United States. Foreign victims are often from Thailand, India, Mexico, Philippines, Haiti, Honduras, El Salvador, and the Dominican Republic—countries where there are poor and vulnerable people.

US citizens are also victims of human trafficking, with the Federal Bureau of Investigation estimating that more than one hundred thousand children and young women are trafficked annually. The children range in age from nine to nineteen, with an average age of eleven. Although most of these children are runaways or throwaways, some come from stable families and are tricked by unscrupulous traffickers. Although human trafficking occurs in every state, the highest numbers of cases occur in Texas, California, New York, and Florida. Victims of human trafficking are typically forced to work as prostitutes, in domestic servitude, in small family-owned businesses, and on farms or in factories.

The viewpoints that follow, which offer various opinions on human trafficking, are arranged in four chapters that address questions concerning the factors that contribute to human trafficking; the role the Internet plays in the business of trafficking; how globalization affects trafficking; and how human trafficking can be stopped.

CHAPTER 1

What Factors Contribute to Human Trafficking?

Chapter Preface

Human trafficking is big business and a significant global problem that victimizes approximately twenty-seven million people and rakes in approximately $32 billion annually. With so many victims, human trafficking cuts across a broad spectrum of social, economic, and political classes. Some of its causes are social, political, or cultural, given that some countries and regions experience conditions that leave their citizens vulnerable to human traffickers. These conditions include poverty, situations of armed conflict, and ethnic or gender discrimination. These conditions often encourage migration to a country or region perceived as having more opportunity. The destabilization of migration leaves people vulnerable to human traffickers. Other causes are more personal. Some people—particularly children—are at risk of being trafficked because they have an unstable family situation or because they are homeless.

One example is that of Natalia, a young girl who was victimized because her family wanted her to escape the poverty of her native country. Born and raised in a small village in Ghana, Natalia had little opportunity for education. A trafficker persuaded Natalia's family to send her to the United States, where she would receive an education while working for a family.

However, soon after Natalia arrived in the United States, she was physically and sexually abused by the father of the family with whom she lived. She was never allowed to enroll in school and worked eighteen hours a day for the next six years cleaning the house and caring for the family's three children.

The story of Ashleigh, as told on the Abolish Child Trafficking website, illustrates how an abandoned child can fall prey to human traffickers.

Ashleigh's father was murdered when she was five, and her mother was a drug addict. After a series of failed placements with a family member and in foster care homes, Ashleigh was living on the streets at the age of fifteen. A stranger gained her confidence then beat and enslaved her. Ashleigh was forced into prostitution, severely beaten, and mistreated by her pimp and customers before she was rescued.

Sometimes even the most unlikely people end up the victims of human trafficking. Theresa Flores, the daughter of an executive, lived in an affluent suburb of Detroit. According to "Theresa's Testimony," on the Traffickfree.com website, she became attracted to the wrong boy at school, who drugged her and raped her the first chance he got. While she was being raped, two of his male relatives took photographs, which they used to blackmail her into submission. For the next two years, Theresa was forced to work as a sex slave. She was tortured psychologically and physically daily. Theresa was forced to have sex with hundreds of men. From time to time, a dead animal would be placed in her mailbox to intimidate her. According to Theresa, "every child is vulnerable in some way, no matter if you live in the inner city of Toledo, Cleveland, Cincinnati, or Columbus, or if you are raised with the best of everything."

As varied as the causes behind human trafficking are, two factors are present in every case: a victim who is vulnerable for some reason and a criminal trafficker motivated by greed. The following chapter presents various viewpoints that address the factors that contribute to human trafficking.

Human Trafficking Is Caused by the Greed of Criminals

United Nations Inter-Agency Project on Human Trafficking

The United Nations Inter-Agency Project on Human Trafficking is an organization with a central focus on trafficking in persons and a mandate to facilitate a stronger and more coordinated response to trafficking in persons in the Greater Mekong Subregion in Asia.

What makes a person or community vulnerable to human trafficking? Common assumptions are that poverty and a lack of education are primary factors, but evidence often proves otherwise. In different locales, different factors increase the risk of being trafficked. Evidence-based programming requires an understanding of the vulnerability factors, verified through research with individuals and communities at risk, to design appropriate interventions and achieve measurable positive impact in preventing trafficking and risky migration.

Many Trafficking Prevention Programs Are Ineffective

Many trafficking prevention programs broadly assume that, no matter the local context, the key vulnerability factors are poverty and lack of knowledge about human trafficking. That is, trafficking prevention interventions often move forward with poverty alleviation programs coupled with awareness raising, without first investigating whether the key drivers of human trafficking in the given area truly are household income or lack of understanding about trafficking and safe migration.

There have been many studies throughout various parts of Asia (and beyond) demonstrating that poverty, low education, and lack of understanding about human trafficking are not necessarily key contributing factors to vulnerability at all. For example, higher education among girls in Northern Thailand has been documented to increase risk of trafficking, since the high opportunity cost of being in school for so long increases the pressures and hopes that girls feel to earn good money and increase their family's social status—leading to unsafe migration and trafficking to Bangkok, Malaysia, and Japan.

We must be careful with our assumptions lest our interventions be wrongly targeted. To date, the impact of most programs aiming to prevent and reduce human trafficking has been low and/or challenging to measure, with a few isolated exceptions. In reality, the attempt to measure real impact from trafficking prevention programs is rare. However, it is clear that many populations thought to be at risk have been saturated with knowledge about the risks of human trafficking by NGOs [nongovernmental organizations], government agencies, and UN [United Nations] programs, but yet thousands in these same awareness-raising areas are still trafficked every year. It is clearly more complicated in many local contexts than simply poverty and lack of knowledge, with clear implications for the effectiveness of poverty alleviation, scholarship, awareness raising, alternative livelihoods, and other prevention interventions.

> It is extremely important to keep in mind that human trafficking involves gross abuses of human rights.

In structural terms, economic disparities between areas, countries and regions constitute the major pull factor for migration. Migration in itself is not synonymous with trafficking, of course, and in fact is an important poverty alleviation strategy in itself. However, mismatches between immigration policies and labor market realities have created a large demand for irregular, unprotected migration, and a pool of people who are highly vulnerable to abuse and exploitation.

Human Traffickers Are Criminals

As well as economic disparity, demographic factors are also leading to spatial differences in demand and supply. As their populations age, economically developed countries require migrant labor, while the increasing number of women desiring to maintain careers outside of the home will continue to increase the demand for foreign domestic labor. Differing sex ratios between neighboring countries and regions (for example, significantly more women than men in Vietnam, with the opposite in rural China) may continue to encourage an increase in cross-border marriages.

At points of origin, unsafe or desperate migration, possibly with a deceitful or exploitative recruiter, can be triggered by any number of factors: illness of a family member leading to a need for quick cash; boredom in the village and piqued interest in the urban life due to television; success stories (whether true or untrue) of returning migrants; inability to access citizenship; loss of land; other external shocks such as droughts or floods.

Ultimately, however, it is extremely important to keep in mind that human trafficking involves gross abuses of human rights, including physical and mental abuse, rape, forced drug use, deprivation of liberties, and sometimes even murder.

Human trafficking is not 'caused' by poverty, lack of education, lack of legal status, or any other vulnerability factor: human trafficking is caused by human traffickers—criminals who commit criminal acts against victims and vulnerable people.

Poverty Is the Root Cause of Human Trafficking

Francesca Petriliggieri

Francesca Petriliggieri is a specialist in public policy at Cáritas Española in Madrid, Spain.

The United Nations estimates nearly 2.5 million people from 127 different countries are being trafficked around the world for forced labour; bonded labour and forced prostitution are the major forms of this phenomenon. It is difficult to determine exactly the magnitude of the problem due to the illegal nature of trafficking, and different kinds of estimates can only give a partial vision of the reality. Annually, according to U.S. Government-sponsored research completed in 2006, approximately 800,000 people are trafficked across national borders, which does not include millions trafficked within their own countries. Approximately 80 percent of transnational victims are women and girls and up to 50 percent are minors.

Poverty Puts People at Risk

In Europe the most known form of trafficking, although it doesn't mean it's the most widespread, is for sexual exploitation: thousands of women and girls are bought, sold and forced into the sex market every year, coming from inside and outside the European borders. Victims from Central and Eastern Europe, as well as from Asia, Africa and Latin America have been identified in the last years, and it seems that we face a growing phenomenon.

Looking for the root causes of trafficking in human beings we can identify some factors which put people, particularly women and children, at risk of falling prey to the traffickers. Except for existing demand, which is fueled by the huge amount of money that traffickers can make, another factor is surely poverty, intended as a "lack of well-being", and composed of different dimensions, as: financial resources, health-related well-being, accommodation, level of education, occupational integration, societal integration, integration regarding laws of residence and family of origin. . . .

People who fall victims of human trafficking often find themselves in vulnerable situations.

Members and colleagues of COATNET (Christian Organizations against Trafficking) . . . expressed their opinions on the correlation between poverty and human trafficking, confirming, from their direct experience with victims all over the world, the importance of poverty as one of the causes or even the major cause of the phenomenon.

The Role of Migration

Even the existing assumption that the most poor don't migrate was denied by Vadym Yatsyshyn, a psychologist from Caritas Ukraine working with trafficked women, who said that even very poor and desperate people manage to borrow funds to pay criminal networks to help them immigrate.

People who fall victims of human trafficking often find themselves in vulnerable situations, which include precarious circumstances in different aspects of their lives, especially in the area of employment, housing conditions and the family configuration. These situations can consist of insecure working conditions, low quality accommodation and residential area and unstable family structures. The dimensions of poverty are interconnected and moving out of a global precarious situation can be very difficult, turning it into a whole life of multiple deprivations. In these circumstances any specific event like an illness, a divorce, the loss of an income, can lead people to seek and take into consideration any solution or possibility of survival. One of the possible solutions for change is obviously migration, and the desire or the decision to migrate lies often at the basis of a human trafficking case....

Why People Take Risks

There are anyway many other factors that play an important role in shaping the situation of vulnerability and making it more complex, among them: economic and social inequality, political instability, gender discrimination and violence, existence and function of social networks. All of these factors are of course strictly related to poverty, intended as a multidimensional and interactive condition.

It's not a coincidence that histories of trafficked women often show previous situations of domestic violence.

In this globalised world disparities and social and economic inequalities are constantly growing, so the gap between people who achieve social welfare and the ones who are doomed to poverty and exclusion widens and becomes more evident every day. This means that not only poverty, but also better life options and the prospect of a more prosperous future are some of the reasons that put people in a more vulnerable situation, pushing them to take risks. The possibility to increase in some way the personal and familiar well-being represents a very strong motivation that, in some cases, doesn't allow seeing clearly the hidden dangers behind what seems a big opportunity.

One of the methods of recruitment most used by traffickers is actually a false offer of employment, which strengthens the idea that poverty and socio-economic inequality are essential root causes of trafficking.

"There is a strong link between poverty, consumerism, levels of skills and inadequate employment opportunities. Disparities brought about by the above factors leading to unequal levels of modernisation and development creates a climate which encourages those with less skills and competence, to take risks and become vulnerable to trafficking," [states] M. Shimray, Caritas India.

The Role of Gender

Nonetheless considering that the majority of victims of human trafficking are women, it is clear that inequality between men and women is also a key factor. Equality between men and women is still far from being achieved in the world, and in some countries women confront major violations of their human rights: feminisation of poverty, discrimination and violence against women are only some examples of this. These situations make women visibly more vulnerable to trafficking and false opportunities. It's not a coincidence that histories of trafficked women often show previous situations of domestic violence.

Giedrė Blažytė, Project Coordinator at Missing Persons' Family Support Centre in Lithuania, underlined how important relations in the family and surrounding community are. "Most of the girls we meet in our work are from the socially marginalised families or grew up in the orphans' home".

The social network, including family members, can be in these cases at the same time a safety mechanism, because it gives protection and information against risky situations or it can be the source of the danger itself, as family members or acquaintances are part of the exploitation network and can put the victim under considerable pressures. Many cases have shown the role of acquaintances in gaining the confidence of the victims and tricking them with false promises. On the other hand people that lack completely a social network and act alone are also very exposed to the danger of human trafficking.

The Need for Education

Should poverty be directly addressed through counter-trafficking projects and activities? "Of course yes,—says Ms [Jindriska] Krpalkova [of Caritas Czech Republic]—but this a difficult question HOW? This issue demands great changes in people's minds and in policy. People should have equal access to education, labour market, medical care, etc.—as we can read it in Universal Declaration of Human Rights. What is not possible in nowadays' world. So, maybe anti-trafficking activities should contain more prevention—such as creating new working possibilities, as to talk about social benefits better addressed allocations, as to target endangered groups, etc."

Economic empowerment would address poverty and lack of local employment opportunities.

"Poverty should be specifically addressed to make the people aware, educated and socially and economically empowered. The Government should develop the policy and plan to uplift the situation of the people at the local levels. The implementation of the policy plan and the laws should be strictly monitored. The Government and NGOs [nongovernmental organizations] should work in close collaboration without duplication. Income Generating Programmes (IGP) that support people to be independent should be developed by utilising the local resources. So that people get all the opportunity and the facilities in their own place. This helps to decrease the migration of the people from their living areas," [states] Rupa Rai, Caritas Nepal.

Omar Mahmoud, who fights trafficking in human beings in Ghana (Friends of Suffering Humanity) also speaks of a greater need for such livelihood programmes, economic support for poor families especially in isolated rural communities. So called Livelihood Programmes could serve as a good intervention to alleviate poverty and consequently reduce the incidence of trafficking in persons in Ghana, "because many try to migrate and don't get safe migration; others sell their children to cope up with their poverty; some allow children to work to service debt (debt bondage) and at times outright sell".

Economic empowerment would address poverty and lack of local employment opportunities. Miroslav Valenta from Caritas Bosnia and Herzegovina speaks of studies which demonstrate that this lack of economic opportunities pushes people to look for work beyond their home communities. By developing programs that offer livelihood options, including basic education, skills training and literacy, especially for women and other traditionally disadvantaged groups, we could increase their economic opportunities and contribute to risk reduction of trafficking.

Erich Ruppen from Caritas Switzerland, believes we should become a better voice speaking of poverty and calling for better response to be heard by the governments and people. We should become stronger advocates and also evaluate, diverse and update our anti-trafficking activities.

"There are emerging trends which reveal that disparity is one important factor that motivates and pushes one to migrate. An important link between poverty and trafficking which suggests a way to reduce the problem is through policy support for legal and safe migration. Safer channels of migration based on clearly drawn out legal provisions for migrants in the sending and receiving countries will help prevent and reduce human trafficking and this needs strong advocacy at national and international levels. In fact, policies that promote legal and safe migration are more likely to have an impact on both poverty reduction and trafficking," [states] M. Shimray, Caritas India.

In conclusion poverty and socio-economic inequalities make the perfect ground for human trafficking to develop and grow. However it's necessary to consider specific contexts and key factors in order to understand the problem deeply and in a comprehensive way, as it links with the issues of migration and growing disparities. This kind of analysis should help private and public institutions and organizations to better address the problem in their interventions.

Poverty Is Only One Factor Contributing to Human Trafficking

Simon Butcher

Simon Butcher is a blogger for Stop the Traffik, a coalition with the goals of raising awareness of human trafficking worldwide, putting an end to the sale of people, prosecuting the traffickers, and aiding the victims.

Last week, the Institute for Trafficked, Exploited and Missing Persons (ITEMP) published a new report identifying poverty as the root cause of human trafficking. "By finding the roots of the problem, we can begin to look for permanent solutions," ITEMP Director of Operations Charles Moore said.

Many Factors Contribute to Human Trafficking

You can perhaps imagine the scene: the worldwide anti-trafficking movement sat together in a grand auditorium as the 'root cause' is announced. The lights go down, the room falls silent as the host opens the golden envelope, announcing . . . "And the root cause of human trafficking is . . . global poverty".

There's some polite clapping and some patting of backs, but the overwhelming feeling in the room is one of slight demoralization. "Well how are we meant to solve global poverty?" they ask each other. "So to stop trafficking we have to eliminate poverty first?" they whisper, disheartened.

It goes without saying that tackling poverty is a massively important cause. But the good news is that combating trafficking *does not* require us to eradicate world poverty.

Myth number 1: "Poverty is the sole cause of human trafficking."

Not only is blaming poverty alone for human trafficking disheartening, it's also misleading and inaccurate. There may be a correlation between the two phenomena, and poverty almost certainly increases an individual's vulnerability to trafficking, but so many other factors come into play too. To name but 5: the approach taken by law enforcement authorities to the issue; the legislative measures taken by national governments; global gender inequalities; the level of access to education; falling in love with the wrong guy . . . Most of these things can be shaped and influenced, and it's up to us to do so.

Myth number 2: "There's not much we can do about such a huge issue."

Yes, it's a huge, global problem, but it's also a local issue. Every case of trafficking starts in a community and ends in a community; every case of trafficking is preventable. The human trafficking industry is thriving because it is so low risk. Every one of us can do something to make the risk to the trafficker higher; to make it impossible for traffickers to hide themselves and their victims. ACT (Active Communities against Trafficking) is a worldwide network of groups tackling human trafficking by doing just that. . . .

Moreover, every one of us can do something to tackle the root causes of trafficking—and it doesn't require you to eradicate world poverty. Through the Freedom Ticket For Life campaign, STOP THE TRAFFIK is supporting community groups in trafficking hotspots around the world. Together, we are increasing access to education, raising awareness of the dangers amongst the most vulnerable, and helping people build lives free from the risk of trafficking. . . .

So often, poverty is presented as a mammoth barrier standing in the way of stopping trafficking. It isn't—there is no barrier—this is a winnable fight.

Race and Ethnicity Make People Vulnerable to Human Trafficking

Jamaal Bell

Jamaal Bell is the editor of Race-Talk.org, a blog and website de-voted to issues surrounding race, gender, equity, and social jus-tice.

I watch and listen to the advocacy of human trafficking at rallies, on web sites, in government reports and NGO [non-governmental organization] reports. The research and statis-tics on human trafficking in America are ambiguous, espe-cially in relation to race and ethnicity. We need to explicitly recognize the connections between trafficking, poverty, migra-tion, gender, racism and racial discrimination to adequately battle and destroy human trafficking in the U.S.

Trafficking persons is inherently discriminatory. Since an overwhelming majority of trafficked persons are women, traf-ficking in most circles is usually considered a gender issue, es-pecially in the United States (majority of trafficking in the U.S. is sex trafficking). In the U.S., most state human traffick-ing laws explicitly and directly address sexual exploitation, ig-noring or vaguely covering other types of trafficking.

However, a link that is rarely discussed in open forums about human trafficking is racial discrimination. A question that I don't hear enough is, "Does race and ethnicity contrib-ute to the likelihood of people becoming victims of traffick-ing?" I say, "Yes." Furthermore, I believe that not only does race and ethnicity constitute a risk factor for trafficking, it may also determine the treatment those victims' experience.

The Polaris Project, who does outstanding work in combating human trafficking, stated the majority of trafficked persons come from vulnerable populations, including undocumented migrants, runaways and at-risk youth, oppressed or marginalized groups, and the poor; specifically because they are easiest to recruit and control. In the U.S., statistically speaking, people of color more than fit this criterion.

Available Statistics by Race

A large majority of trafficked persons in the U.S. for the purposes of labor and sexual exploitation are people of color. Domestically, 50 percent of trafficked victims are children and overwhelmingly are girls, according to the U.S. Department of Justice.

Most foreign nationals are women, children and men from Mexico and East Asia, as well as from South Asia, Central America, Africa, and Europe, about 17,500 each year, according to statistics complied by Polaris Project and 2009 TIP [Trafficking in Persons] report.

Seventy-seven percent of victims in alleged human trafficking incidents reported in the U.S. were people of color, according to a Bureau of Justice Statistics Report [BJS]. An example of BJS's ambiguity is that 747 out of 1,442 reported incidents recorded no racial or ethnic origin.

Racism is deeply embedded in human trafficking and must be racially inclusive and explicitly included in its literature, statistics and advocacy. To combat this modern-day slavery, the trafficking cycle should recognize explicitly the connections between trafficking, migration, poverty, racism, gender and racial discrimination.

We need to urge and support our NGOs, national and state governments to adequately report trafficking incidents. It is important to know the origin of the victims and the suspected traffickers, race and ethnic backgrounds to better understand the vulnerabilities and how traffickers exploit opportunities.

I am advocating that we remove and uncover the ambiguity of the characteristics of trafficked persons and the traffickers and be explicit about who they are and what populations in America are most affected so we can make specific and measurable progress. The notion that anyone can be a victim of human trafficking is true, however, the fact that the majority of victims are people of color should not be undermined or understated.

CHAPTER 2

Should Internet Sites Used for Sex Trafficking Be Shut Down?

Overview: The Role of the Internet in Human Trafficking

Mark Latonero

Mark Latonero is research director of the Center on Communication Leadership & Policy at the University of Southern California's Annenberg School for Communication and Journalism.

Research on the role of the Internet and technology in facilitating human trafficking is emerging and not yet comprehensive. Researchers have examined the increased use of the Internet by traffickers and the new challenges technology presents, especially concerning the sexual exploitation of children. A literature review conducted for this report did not find any research addressing labor trafficking online.

The Internet Facilitates Sex Trafficking

Donna Hughes, an American researcher on trafficking of women and children, has studied how the Internet has facilitated the global trafficking industry since 1997. She notes how closely trafficking, especially sex trafficking, is intertwined with new technologies. According to Hughes, "The sexual exploitation of women and children is a global human rights crisis that is being escalated by the use of new technologies."

Researchers have analyzed the link between new technologies and human trafficking and explored the possible advantages the Internet provides for traffickers. For example, a group of experts commissioned by the Council of Europe found that "the Internet industry and the sex industry are closely inter-

Mark Latonero, "Background," *Human Trafficking Online: The Role of Social Networking Sites and Online Classifieds*, pp. 10–15. Los Angeles: University of Southern California Center on Communication Leadership & Policy, September 2011, Copyright © 2011 by Mark Latonero. All rights reserved. Reproduced by permission.

linked and the scope, volume, and content of the material on the Internet promoting or enacting trafficking in human beings for the purpose of sexual exploitation . . . are unprecedented."

Studies have examined the role of online technologies in the recruiting or grooming of children by traffickers.

A Shared Hope International [SHI] report offers a comparison of the marketplace of commercial sexual exploitation in four countries and describes the Internet as a major impetus behind the growth of the sex trade, noting, "Technology has become the single greatest facilitator of the commercial sex trade in all of the countries observed, with the exception of Jamaica, where word of mouth continues to dominate." According to the report, "As one of the most technologically advanced countries in the world, the U.S. faces the challenge of combating facilitation of sex tourism and sex trafficking markets by technology." The same report included a Google search by SHI for sites associated with sex trafficking. The web analysis identified more than 5,000 "suspected" websites that directly or indirectly facilitate the sex trafficking and sex tourism industry.

However, identifying incidences of human trafficking is not straightforward. In a report for the Council of Europe, researchers conducted an Internet search for potential trafficking sites and emphasized that a website can only be termed "suspect," since there is no evidence that the girls featured in ads for sex services or marriage are in fact trafficking victims. What is clear is that the Internet has changed the methods used to recruit and market victims, and it has "certainly contributed to the rise of trafficking in human beings."

There are many examples of research addressing the online safety of children and the risk of sexual exploitation. Studies have examined the role of online technologies in the recruiting or grooming of children by traffickers. An SHI report on domestic minor sex trafficking in America notes that the Internet is not only used to advertise sexual services, but that "pimps, madams, and escort agencies recruit new members through their own websites, Myspace accounts, and Facebook accounts." The role of social networking sites was the focus of a recent report by the Australian Institute of Criminology, which found that "social networking sites, in particular, have become an important element in the child grooming process. These technologies, popular with the digital/virtual generation, allow offenders to make contact with children and even masquerade as children in cyberspace to secure their trust and cooperation." An August 2010 report to Congress by the Department of Justice also addressed crimes related to child exploitation and the Internet. According to the report:

> Some criminals have turned away from illicit activities such as drug dealing and robbery toward child sex trafficking, from which they can generate potentially several thousand dollars per day, as a single child can generate as much as $1,000 on a weekend night. In fact, the profitability of child prostitutes to the pimp has increased as Internet advertising and web-enabled cellphones have aided pimps in reaching a larger client base; they can schedule more sexual encounters per child.

The Internet is used not only by traffickers but also by victims and clients. A report on the commercial sexual exploitation of minors in New York City said, "Some teens (23%) said that the Internet was an increasingly popular option to meet customers, and 11% of the teens used the popular website Craigslist to meet prospective 'dates.'" A June 2011 Congressional Research Service report on domestic minor sex trafficking found that the Internet has facilitated the demand for child sex trafficking because it "can rapidly connect buyers of commercial sex with trafficking victims while simultaneously distancing the perpetrator from the criminal transactions."

A Difficult Problem to Measure

However, the exact numbers of children sexually exploited through the Internet are difficult to measure. A 2010 study prepared by the Schapiro Group for the Women's Funding Network details the results of several statewide studies of commercial sexual exploitation of female children in the United States. The results indicate a significant number of girls under age 18 are involved in the sex trade, with rates varying state by state.

Although the study presents original research addressing the use of Internet classified advertisements in the commercial sexual exploitation of children, major components of the report lack methodological rigor. As a result, some of the methods employed in the study—specifically, the method of determining juvenile prostitutes by counting pictures of young-looking women online—were publicly criticized. Despite the shortcomings of the Women's Funding Network study, it gained considerable attention in September 2010 when it was introduced in congressional testimony addressing the issue of domestic minor sex trafficking.

The Berkman Center for Internet & Society created the Internet Safety Technical Task Force, which includes major social networking sites, communication companies, and scholars, to analyze social networking sites and their efforts to increase online safety for children. The results indicate that social networking sites are making an effort to increase online safety for children and that there is potential for future technological solutions. The task force emphasized that "more research specifically needs to be done concerning the activities of sex offenders on social network sites and other online environments, and encourages law enforcement to work with researchers to make more data available for this purpose."

The Australian Institute of Criminology echoed the need for collaboration, stating, "A future solution in fighting child exploitation, and perhaps human trafficking as a whole, requires effective coordination and collaboration on the part of a wide range of government and private sector entities."

Ads on Websites Contribute to Human Trafficking

Marsha Blackburn and Carolyn Maloney

Marsha Blackburn is a member of the US House of Representatives from Tennessee. Carolyn Maloney is a member of the US House of Representatives from New York.

A s Members of Congress committed to combating all forms of human trafficking, we write to you with concerns about reports of Google's advertising practices. Recently, dozens of human rights groups called on the National Association of Attorneys General to investigate Google's advertising practices that these groups believe contribute to the problem of human trafficking in America and globally.

Ads on Google Promote Human Trafficking

Whatever Google is doing or is not doing to prevent these sorts of advertisements from appearing on their properties, Google has not satisfied a significant number of human rights organizations who have a specialized understanding of how these ads contribute to the human trafficking of women and girls. We are particularly concerned that these human rights groups may have identified yet another area where Google profits from illicit activities such as Google's advertising of controlled substances for which your company paid a $500,000,000 forfeiture to the United States last year.

Accordingly, we request that you provide us with answers to the following initial questions we have regarding these developments:

Marsha Blackburn and Carolyn Maloney, "Letter to Larry Page, Chief Executive Officer of Google," April 3, 2012.

1. Apart from Google's donations to large human rights organizations, what is your company doing internally to ensure that sexually exploitative advertisements do not appear?

2. What is Google's stated internal policy regarding exploitative advertising? What evidence do you have that those policies are being complied with by both Google's internal and external advertising sales teams?

3. What steps does Google take to instruct its advertising sales managers, consultants, and other employees regarding the evaluation of advertisers of such exploitative marketing?

4. If Google were to determine that it profits from such advertising, what steps would you take to ensure those profits were publicly disclosed and then disgorged? Would that process require restating Google's earnings for past securities filings?

Online markets provide traffickers with the ability to reach untold customers across all political jurisdictions. As a global leader and innovator in internet technologies, Google is in a unique position to do its part to fight human exploitation and trafficking, and we would encourage the company to proactively address these concerns.

We look forward to your reply and to engaging with Google cooperatively to stop human trafficking in America and around the world.

Underage Girls Are Marketed for Prostitution on Classified Advertising Websites

Nicholas D. Kristof

Nicholas D. Kristof is a Pulitzer Prize-winning columnist for The New York Times.

I went on a walk in Manhattan the other day with a young woman who once had to work these streets, hired out by eight pimps while she was just 16 and 17. She pointed out a McDonald's where pimps sit while monitoring the girls outside, and a building where she had repeatedly been ordered online as if she were a pizza.

Young Sex Trafficking Victims Are Sold on Backpage

Alissa, her street name, escaped that life and is now a 24-year-old college senior planning to become a lawyer—but she will always have a scar on her cheek where a pimp gouged her with a potato peeler as a warning not to escape. "Like cattle owners brand their cattle," she said, fingering her cheek, "he wanted to brand me in a way that I would never forget."

After Alissa testified against her pimps, six of them went to prison for up to 25 years. Yet these days, she reserves her greatest anger not at pimps but at companies that enable them. She is particularly scathing about Backpage.com, a classified advertising Web site that is used to sell auto parts, furniture, boats—and girls. Alissa says pimps routinely peddled her on Backpage.

"You can't buy a child at Wal-Mart, can you?" she asked me. "No, but you can go to Backpage and buy me on Backpage."

Backpage accounts for about 70 percent of prostitution advertising among five Web sites that carry such ads in the United States, earning more than $22 million annually from prostitution ads, according to AIM Group, a media research and consulting company. It is now the premier Web site for human trafficking in the United States, according to the National Association of Attorneys General. And it's not a fly-by-night operation. Backpage is owned by Village Voice Media, which also owns the estimable *Village Voice* newspaper.

It is "shortsighted, ill-informed and counterproductive" to focus on Backpage when many other Web sites are also involved.

Attorneys general from 48 states have written a joint letter to Village Voice Media, pleading with it to get out of the flesh trade. An online petition at Change.org has gathered 94,000 signatures asking Village Voice Media to stop taking prostitution advertising. Instead, the company has used *The Village Voice* to mock its critics. Alissa thought about using her real name for this article but decided not to for fear that *Village Voice* would retaliate.

Court records and public officials back Alissa's account, and there is plenty of evidence that underage girls are marketed on Backpage. Arrests in such cases have been reported in at least 22 states.

Just this month, prosecutors in New York City filed charges in a case involving a gang that allegedly locked a 15-year-old Long Island girl in an empty house, drugged her, tied her up, raped her, and advertised her on Backpage. After a week of being sold for sex, prosecutors in Queens said, the girl escaped.

Liz McDougall, general counsel of Village Voice Media, told me that it is "shortsighted, ill-informed and counterproductive" to focus on Backpage when many other Web sites are also involved, particularly because Backpage tries to screen out ads for minors and reports possible trafficking cases to the authorities. McDougall denied that Backpage dominates the field and said that the Long Island girl was marketed on 13 other Web sites as well. But if street pimps go to jail for profiteering on under-age girls, should their media partners like Village Voice Media really get a pass?

Shutting Down Backpage Will Hurt Pimps

Paradoxically, *Village Voice* began as an alternative newspaper to speak truth to power. It publishes some superb journalism. So it's sad to see it accept business from pimps in the greediest and most depraved kind of exploitation.

True, many prostitution ads on Backpage are placed by adult women acting on their own without coercion; they're not my concern. Other ads are placed by pimps: the Brooklyn district attorney's office says that the great majority of the sex trafficking cases it prosecutes involve girls marketed on Backpage.

Alissa, who grew up in a troubled household in Boston, has a story that is fairly typical. She says that one night when she was 16—and this matches the account she gave federal prosecutors—a young man approached her and told her she was attractive. She thought that he was a rapper, and she was flattered. He told her that he wanted her to be his girlfriend, she recalls wistfully.

Within a few weeks, he was prostituting her—even as she continued to study as a high school sophomore. Alissa didn't run away partly because of a feeling that there was a romantic bond, partly because of Stockholm syndrome [wherein hostages begin to side with their captors], and partly because of raw fear. She says violence was common if she tried connecting to the outside world or if she didn't meet her daily quota for cash.

"He would get aggressive and strangle me and physically assault me and threaten to sell me to someone that was more violent than him, which he eventually did," Alissa recalled. She said she was sold from one pimp to another several times, for roughly $10,000 each time.

She was sold to johns seven days a week, 365 days a year. After a couple of years, she fled, but a pimp tracked her down and—with the women he controlled—beat and stomped Alissa, breaking her jaw and several ribs, she said. That led her to cooperate with the police.

There are no simple solutions to end sex trafficking, but it would help to have public pressure on Village Voice Media to stop carrying prostitution advertising. The Film Forum has already announced that it will stop buying ads in *The Village Voice*. About 100 advertisers have dropped Rush Limbaugh's radio show because of his demeaning remarks about women. Isn't it infinitely more insulting to provide a forum for the sale of women and girls?

Let's be honest: Backpage's exit from prostitution advertising wouldn't solve the problem, for smaller Web sites would take on some of the ads. But it would be a setback for pimps to lose a major online marketplace. When Craigslist stopped taking such ads in 2010, many did not migrate to new sites: online prostitution advertising plummeted by more than 50 percent, according to AIM Group.

Alissa, who now balances her college study with part-time work at a restaurant and at Fair Girls, an antitrafficking organization, deserves the last word. "For a Web site like Backpage to make $22 million off our backs," she said, "it's like going back to slave times."

Restricting Classified Advertising Websites Helps Pimps and Human Traffickers

Danah Boyd

Danah Boyd is a senior researcher at Microsoft Corporation, a research assistant professor at New York University, a visiting researcher at Harvard Law School, a fellow at Harvard's Berkman Center, and an adjunct associate professor at the University of New South Wales.

For the last 12 years, I've dedicated immense amounts of time, money and energy to end violence against women and children. As a victim of violence myself, I'm deeply committed to destroying any institution or individual leveraging the sex-power matrix that results in child trafficking, nonconsensual prostitution, domestic violence and other abuses. If I believed that censoring Craigslist would achieve these goals, I'd be the first in line to watch them fall. But from the bottom of my soul and the depths of my intellect, I believe that the current efforts to censor Craigslist's "adult services" achieves the absolute opposite. Rather than helping those who are abused, it fundamentally helps pimps, human traffickers and others who profit off of abusing others.

Shutting Down Craigslist Was Counterproductive

On Friday, under tremendous pressure from US attorneys general and public advocacy groups, Craigslist shut down its "Adult Services" section. There is little doubt that this space has been used by people engaged in all sorts of illicit activities, many of which result in harmful abuses. But the debate that has ensued has centered on the wrong axis, pitting protecting the abused against freedom of speech. What's implied in public discourse is that protecting potential victims requires censorship; thus, anti-censorship advocates are up in arms attacking regulators for trying to curtail First Amendment rights. While I am certainly a proponent of free speech online, I find it utterly depressing that these groups fail to see how this is actually an issue of transparency, not free speech. And how this does more to hurt potential victims than help.

Most ISPs have a fundamental business—if not moral—interest in helping protect people.

If you've ever met someone who is victimized through trafficking or prostitution, you'll hear a pretty harrowing story about what it means to be invisible and powerless, feeling like no one cares and no one's listening. Human trafficking and most forms of abusive prostitution exist in a black market, with corrupt intermediaries making connections and offering "protection" to those who they abuse for profit. The abused often have no recourse, either because their movements are heavily regulated (as with those trafficked) or because they're violating the law themselves (as with prostitutes).

The Internet has changed the dynamics of prostitution and trafficking, making it easier for prostitutes and traffickers to connect with clients without too many layers of intermediaries. As a result, the Internet has become an intermediary, often without the knowledge of those internet service providers (ISPs) who are the conduits. This is what makes people believe that they should go after ISPs like Craigslist. Faulty logic suggests that if Craigslist is effectively a digital pimp who's profiting off of online traffic, why shouldn't it be prosecuted as such?

The problem with this logic is that it fails to account for three important differences: 1) most ISPs have a fundamental business—if not moral—interest in helping protect people; 2) the visibility of illicit activities online makes it much easier to get at, and help, those who are being victimized; and 3) a one-stop-shop is more helpful for law enforcement than for criminals. In short, Craigslist is not a pimp, but a public perch from which law enforcement can watch without being seen.

Internet Service Providers Have a Fundamental Business Interest in Helping People

When Internet companies profit off of online traffic, they need their clients to value them and the services they provide. If companies can't be trusted—especially when money is exchanging hands—they lose business. This is especially true for companies that support peer-to-peer exchange of money and goods. This is what motivates services like eBay and Amazon to make it very easy for customers to get refunded when ripped off. Craigslist has made its name and business on helping people connect around services, and while there are plenty of people who use its openness to try to abuse others, Craigslist is deeply committed to reducing fraud and abuse. It's not always successful—no company is. And the more freedom that a company affords, the more room for abuse. But what makes Craigslist especially beloved is that it is run by people who truly want to make the world a better place and who are deeply committed to a healthy civic life.

If you live a privileged life, your exposure to prostitution may be limited to made-for-TV movies.

I have always been in awe of Craig Newmark, Craigslist's founder and now a "customer service rep" with the company. He's made a pretty penny off of Craigslist, so what's he doing with it? Certainly not basking in the Caribbean sun. He's dedicated his life to public service, working with organizations like Sunlight Foundation to increase government accountability and using his resources and networks to help out countless organizations like Donors Choose, Kiva, Consumer Reports and Iraq/Afghani Vets of America. This is the villain behind Craigslist trying to pimp out abused people?

Craigslist is in a tremendous position to actually work *with* law enforcement, both because it's in their economic interests and because the people behind it genuinely want to do good in this world. This isn't an organization dedicated to profiting off of criminals, hosting servers in corrupt political regimes to evade responsibility. This is an organization with both the incentives and interest to actually help. And they have a long track record of doing so.

Visibility Makes It Easier to Help Victims

If you live a privileged life, your exposure to prostitution may be limited to made-for-TV movies and a curious dip into the red-light district of Amsterdam. You are most likely lucky enough to never have known someone who was forced into prostitution, let alone someone who was sold by or stolen from their parents as a child. Perhaps if you live in San Francisco or Las Vegas, you know a high-end escort who has freely chosen her life and works for an agency or lives in a community where she's highly supported. Truly consensual prostitutes do exist, but the vast majority of prostitution is nonconsensual, either through force or desperation. And, no matter how many hip-hop songs try to imply otherwise, the vast majority of pimps are abusive, manipulative, corrupt, addicted bastards. To be fair, I will acknowledge that these scumbags are typically from abusive environments where they too are forced into their profession through circumstances that are unimaginable to most middle class folks. But I still don't believe that this justifies their role in continuing the cycle of abuse.

Along comes the Internet, exposing you to the underbelly of the economy, making visible the sex-power industry that makes you want to vomit. Most people see such cesspools online and imagine them to be the equivalent of a crack house opening up in their gated community. Let's try a different metaphor. Why not think of it instead as a documentary movie happening in real time where you can actually do something about it?

The increased availability of data is not the problem; it's a godsend for getting at the root of the problem and actually helping people.

Visibility is one of the trickiest issues in advocacy. Anyone who's worked for a nonprofit knows that getting people to care is really, really hard. Movies are made in the hopes that people will watch them and do something about the issues presented. Protests and marathons are held in the hopes of bringing awareness to a topic. But there's nothing like the awareness that can happen when it's in your own backyard. And this is why advocates spend a lot of time trying to bring issues home to people.

Visibility serves many important purposes in advocacy. Not only does it motivate people to act, but it also shines a spotlight on every person involved in the issue at hand. In the case of nonconsensual prostitution and human trafficking, this means that those who are engaged in these activities aren't so deeply underground as to be invisible. They're right there. And while they feel protected by the theoretical power of anonymity and the belief that no one can physically approach and arrest them, they're leaving traces of all sorts that make them far easier to find than most underground criminals.

Law Enforcement Can Make Online Spaces Risky for Criminals

Law enforcement is always struggling to gain access to underground networks in order to go after the bastards who abuse people for profit. Underground enforcement is really difficult, and it takes a lot of time to invade a community and build enough trust to get access to information that will hopefully lead to the dens of sin. While it always looks so easy on TV, there's nothing easy or pretty about this kind of work. The Internet has given law enforcement more data than they even know what to do with, more information about more people engaged in more horrific abuses than they've ever been able to obtain through underground work. It's far too easy to mistake more data for more crime and too many aspiring governors use the increase of data to spin the public into a frenzy about the dangers of the Internet. The increased availability of data is not the problem; it's a godsend for getting at the root of the problem and actually helping people.

Censoring Craigslist will do absolutely nothing to help those being victimized, but it will do a lot to help those profiting off of victimization.

When law enforcement is ready to go after a criminal network, they systematically set up a sting, trying to get as many people as possible, knowing that whoever they have underground will immediately lose access the moment they act. The Internet changes this dynamic, because it's a whole lot easier to be underground online, to invade networks and build trust, to go after people one at a time, to grab victims as they're being victimized. It's a lot easier to set up stings online, posing as buyers or sellers and luring scumbags into making the wrong move. All without compromising informants.

Working with ISPs to collect data and doing systematic online stings can make an online space more dangerous for criminals than for victims because this process erodes the trust in the intermediary, the online space. Eventually, law enforcement stings will make a space uninhabitable for criminals by making it too risky for them to try to operate there. Censoring a space may hurt the ISP but it does absolutely nothing to hurt the criminals. Making a space uninhabitable by making it risky for criminals to operate there—and publicizing it—is far more effective. This, by the way, is the core lesson that [former mayor Rudy] Giuliani's crew learned in New York. The problem with this plan is that it requires funding law enforcement.

Using the Internet to Combat the Sex-Power Industry

It makes me scream when I think of how many resources have been used attempting to censor Craigslist instead of leveraging it as a space for effective law enforcement. During the height of the moral panic over sexual predators on MySpace, I had the fortune of spending a lot of time with a few FBI folks and talking to a whole lot of local law enforcement. I learned a scary reality about criminal activity online. Folks in law enforcement know about a lot more criminal activity than they have the time to pursue. Sure, they focus on the big players, going after the massive collectors of child pornography who are most likely to be sex offenders than spending time on the small-time abusers. But it was the medium-time criminals that gnawed at them. They were desperate for more resources so that they could train more law enforcers, pursue more cases, and help more victims. The Internet had made it a lot easier for them to find criminals, but that didn't make their jobs any easier because they were now aware of how many more victims they were unable to help. Most law enforcement in this area are really there because they want to help people and it kills them when they can't help everyone.

There's a lot more political gain to be had demonizing profitable companies than demanding more money be spent (and thus, more taxes be raised) supporting the work that law enforcement does. Taking something that is visible and making it invisible makes a politician look good, even if it does absolutely nothing to help the victims who are harmed. It creates the illusion of safety, while signaling to pimps, traffickers, and other scumbags that their businesses are perfectly safe as long as they stay invisible. Sure, many of these scumbags have an incentive to be as visible as possible to reach as many possible clients as possible, and so they will move on and invade a new service where they can reach clients. And they'll make that ISP's life hell by putting them in the spotlight. And maybe they'll choose an offshore one that American law enforcement can do nothing about. Censorship online is nothing more than whack-a-mole, pushing the issue elsewhere or more underground.

Censoring Craigslist will do absolutely nothing to help those being victimized, but it will do a lot to help those profiting off of victimization. Censoring Craigslist will also create new jobs for pimps and other corrupt intermediaries, since it'll temporarily make it a whole lot harder for individual scumbags to find clients. This will be particularly devastating for the low-end prostitutes who were using Craigslist to escape violent pimps. Keep in mind that occasionally getting beaten up by a scary John is often a whole lot more desirable for many than the regular physical, psychological, and economic abuse they receive from their pimps. So while it'll make it temporarily harder for clients to get access to abusive services, nothing good will come out of it in the long run.

If you want to end human trafficking, if you want to combat nonconsensual prostitution, if you care about the victims of the sex-power industry, don't cheer Craigslist's censorship. This did nothing to combat the cycle of abuse. What we desperately need are more resources for law enforcement to leverage the visibility of the Internet to go after the scumbags who abuse. What we desperately need are for sites like Craigslist to be encouraged to work with law enforcement and help create channels to actually help victims. What we need are innovative citizens who leverage new opportunities to devise new ways of countering abusive industries. We need to take this moment of visibility and embrace it, leverage it to create change, leverage it to help those who are victimized and lack the infrastructure to get help. What you see online should haunt you. But it should drive you to address the core problem by finding and helping victims, not looking for new ways to blindfold yourself. Please, I beg you, don't close your eyes. We need you.

Shutting Down the Adult Services Sections of Classified Advertising Websites Is a Violation of Free Speech

Matt Zimmerman

Matt Zimmerman is a senior staff attorney with the Electronic Frontier Foundation who specializes in issues related to free speech, civil liberties, and privacy law.

On Saturday [September 4, 2010], after years of pressure from law enforcement officials, Internet classified ad web site Craigslist bowed to demands to remove its "Adult Services" section which critics charged encouraged prostitution and other sex-related crimes. Or at least it appears that it did. Without explanation, following the latest in a series of open letters from state attorneys general [AGs] decrying the third party content permitted on the site, Craigslist replaced the "Adult Services" link that formerly appeared on the front page of the site with a white-on-black "censored" bar. Whether this move will substantially affect the rate of illegal prostitution across the country remains to be seen. Many, even some of Craigslist's critics, appear to have their doubts. If nothing else, however, this latest turn in the AGs v. Craigslist saga underscores the misguided nature of the AGs' tactics as well as the fundamental disagreement that we (and Congress) have with the AGs' vision of how the Internet should operate.

Lawbreakers, Not Intermediaries, Should Be Prosecuted

Through this now years-long struggle, Craigslist's legal position has been and remains absolutely, unequivocally correct: the Communications Decency Act of 1996 (or CDA) grants providers of "interactive computer services" an absolute shield against state criminal law liability stemming from material posted by third parties. Put simply, the law ensures that the virtual soapbox is not liable for what the speaker says: merely creating a forum in which users post ads that may violate state law plainly does not lead to liability for a web site operator.

Attorneys general . . . and other law enforcement officers have shown little regard for what the law actually requires.

The federal statutory immunity upon which Craigslist relies is not some clever loophole. Rather, the intermediary immunity provided by the CDA represents a conscious policy decision by Congress to protect individuals and companies who would otherwise be vulnerable targets to litigants who want to silence speech to which they object, illegal or not. We agree with Congress that a federal policy of holding lawbreakers liable for their own illegal behavior instead of holding intermediaries responsible for the illegal acts of others is the right one, both as a matter of fairness as well as an effective strategy by which speech and innovation can be encouraged and rewarded.

This clear protection plays an essential role in how the Internet functions today, protecting every interactive web site operator—from Facebook to Craigslist to the average solo blog operator—from potentially crippling legal bills and liability stemming from comments or other material posted to web sites by third parties. Moreover, if they were obligated to prescreen their users' content, wide swaths of First Amendment-protected speech would inevitably be sacrificed as web site operators, suddenly transformed into conservative content reviewers, permitted only the speech that they could be sure would not trigger lawsuits (or intimidating visits from the attorney general). The ability to encourage speech of all sorts without fear of legal reprisal is a feature of the CDA 230 [Section 230 of the Communications Decency Act] world, not a shortcoming, one that encourages the publication of a diverse range of viewpoints and not just those of rich and cautious media companies who can afford the financial risk of publication.

As the chief law enforcement officers of their respective states, the attorneys general certainly know that their legal threats are completely meritless. Yet these and other law enforcement officers have shown little regard for what the law actually requires and have instead embarked on a vigorous campaign to strong-arm a company into submission based on bogus legal threats that nonetheless play well to many of their constituents. This strategy might amount to good politics, especially in an election year, but it continues to show remarkable disdain for the bedrock legal principles that have largely served the Internet well over the past 15 years.

Craigslist Has Been Cooperative

It didn't have to be this way. Over the past two years, Craigslist repeatedly offered to go far above and beyond their legal obligations to work with law enforcement officials, offering to manually screen ads, require working phone and credit card numbers from ad posters (thereby creating digital footprints by which lawbreakers could be tracked), and help identify missing persons. Not surprisingly, however, having offered to do more than the law required but less than the AGs demanded, the AGs kept coming back for more, some flatly stating that the essential protections offered by CDA 230 should be repealed.

At least two lessons can be drawn from this latest skirmish in the battle between Craigslist and its critics. First, there sadly appears to be little upside to working with many of these law enforcement officials to resolve such important Internet policy disagreements. At each step of this public debate, the AGs have inevitably rewarded completely voluntary, non-mandatory offers of cooperation from Craigslist with further demands and insults. What possible motivation will other companies have to work with law enforcement to address similar concerns in the future?

Second, and more importantly, supporters of the First Amendment should loudly voice their opposition to this type of misguided rhetoric from elected officials. While Craigslist may have "voluntarily" shuttered its Adult Services section, they did so under constant threat from government officials who continually promised meritless lawsuits and even criminal prosecution if their target did not comply. No one (including Craigslist) disputes that sex trafficking is a reprehensible practice that should be vigorously opposed. The dispute lies in whether law enforcement officials should be permitted to bully and dragoon private web site operators into becoming de facto [in reality] censors. Many, including EFF [Electronic Frontier Foundation], profoundly disagree with the prospect of such a reimagined Internet, and the AGs at minimum owe it to the public to be honest about the First Amendment impact of what they are proposing.

Shutting Down the Adult Services Sections of Classified Advertising Websites Will Harm Adult Sex Workers

Kayley Whalen

Kayley Whalen is a development associate at the American Humanist Association.

Attention to the issue of sex trafficking in the United States has risen dramatically over the last few years to the point of a moral panic.

As defined by the Department of Health and Human Services, "sex trafficking is a modern-day form of slavery in which a commercial sex act is induced by force, fraud, or coercion, or in which the person induced to perform such an act is under the age of eighteen years." Statistics for trafficking victims are hard to determine given the shadowy, illegal nature of the practice; however, misconstrued figures, religious and celebrity-endorsed campaigns, and media outlets hungry for a good story have fueled a national hysteria. And the blame for the perceived epidemic has been placed squarely on the shoulders of online advertisers who offer adult service ads, namely Craigslist and Backpage.com, the online classified site owned by Village Voice Media (VVM).

Groundswell's Campaign Is Misguided

In September 2010, after several murders were linked to adult ads on Craigslist, the site announced it would ban sex-related advertising in the United States (in truth, the ads are still there, just well hidden). A year later, Auburn Theological Seminary launched a "social action initiative" called Groundswell which began what they called a multi-faith campaign to target Backpage.com's adult services section. This included an open letter to VVM published in the *New York Times* on October 25, 2011. The letter was signed by prominent religious and moral leaders (including Harvard Humanist Chaplain Greg Epstein), and claimed the backing of fifty-one state attorneys general.

Child sex trafficking destroys lives and is a complete affront to any reasonable understanding of human ethics and morality.

The apparent groundswell of support for Groundswell's campaign can be traced back to a 2009 paper from two University of Pennsylvania professors stating that "an estimated 100,000–300,000 American children are at risk for becoming victims of commercial sexual exploitation." Runaways and those living near an international border were among those considered at risk. The actor Ashton Kutcher, who with his wife Demi Moore started a foundation to combat child sex trafficking, then misreported the figure as fact in an interview on CNN with Piers Morgan in April 2011.

"There's between 100,000 and 300,000 child sex slaves in the United States today," Kutcher stated. "If you don't do something to stop that—that's when there's something wrong with you." With the help of other celebrities, they then launched a Public Service Announcement [PSA] campaign called "Real Men Don't Buy Girls." These PSA's led to an explosion of mainstream media and blog discussions across the United States and helped launch thousands of activists eager to stop the supposed child sex-trafficking epidemic. Enter Groundswell and their campaign against online adult services advertising.

It goes without saying that child sex trafficking destroys lives and is a complete affront to any reasonable understanding of human ethics and morality. Yet Groundswell's campaign is fueled by scare tactics with very little basis in real facts, is an assault on free speech, and is against the best interests of actual sex workers who use online services to conduct business in a much safer and more regulated fashion than other forms of sex work.

At stake here is more than a question of free speech, this is a question of morality—of the best way to avoid human suffering and lives lost.

Unlike Craigslist, VVM has mounted a much stronger defense, claiming to have spent millions of dollars implementing policies and monitoring services to ensure that Backpage.com is adults-only. In a July 2011 article in the *Village Voice* they stated:

> Not only do we have security specialists making constant searches for keywords that might indicate an underage user, but we're quick to cooperate with law enforcement and the National Center for Missing and Exploited Children [NCMEC] when we find suspicious ads. In some cases, our reports about suspicious ads have resulted in underage runaways being traced and recovered—as opposed to the underground economy of bus stations and street corners where kids are truly invisible. Backpage's 123 employees, who screen about 20,000 ads every day, alert NCMEC when they find something suspicious, who in turn contacts law enforcement. That process triggered 230 reports last month.

Transgender Women, Poverty and Sex Work

It is a sad reality that a very high percentage of transgender women, especially transgender women of color, depend on sex work for their very survival, a phenomenon that has long been studied by organizations such as the Sylvia Rivera Law Project in New York City, and the TransHealth Information Project in Philadelphia. And in 2011 the National Gay and Lesbian Task Force (NGLTF) and the National Center for Transgender Equality (NCTE) released a massive, scientifically rigorous survey of transgender and gender nonconforming individuals across the country, which found that 16 percent of those individuals had engaged in the "underground economy"—defined as sex work or dealing drugs—at some point in their lives. Survey participants were also four times as likely to live in extreme poverty than the general population, and 47 percent had either been fired from a job, not hired, or denied a promotion because of their transgender or gender non-conforming identity.

As a humanist, as a transgender woman, and as a sex-worker advocate, I stand with Backpage.com and am opposed to any call for them to remove the adult services section from their website. As a U.S. company, Backpage.com has a right to free speech protected by the First Amendment, and their adult services section is in full compliance with the Communications Decency Act of 1996 (or CDA). But at stake here is more than a question of free speech, this is a question of morality—of the best way to avoid human suffering and lives lost. I firmly believe that the adult services section provides an invaluable service to sex workers desperately in need of a safer and more regulated way to conduct business.

While I believe there is nothing inherently "wrong" with sex work, those who depend on it to provide the basic necessities for life often have been left with no other option because of societal oppression. The Prostitutes Education Network estimates that 1 percent of women have engaged in sex work at some point, and every study of transgender women, including the aforementioned NGLTF/NCTE report, has found a much higher rate among transgender women. Moreover, attempts to stop sex work simply drive it deeper underground, leading to a higher risk of violence, HIV/AIDS, drug abuse, and other dangers.

Of course it's important to address the root of the societal oppression that leads many transgender women and other individuals to sex work, but it's naive to think that such oppression will disappear anytime soon. Getting rid of the adult services section of Backpage.com would be a major step backward from the goal of protecting sex workers, and instead I think stricter regulations and protections can be put in place there. Likewise, to combat the practice of child sex trafficking, we should look to ameliorate the conditions of adolescents deemed at risk.

Harm Reduction Strategies for Adult Sex Workers

In 2007 I volunteered at a harm reduction organization called Trans Health Information Project (TIP), which is based out of inner-city Philadelphia and serves hundreds of transgender and gender non-conforming clients who are largely homeless and/or living in poverty—almost all of whom depend on some kind of sex work to survive. We provided HIV testing, counseling, safe-sex supplies, syringe-exchange (both for IV drug users and also for trans individuals who injected silicone and/or hormones), legal counseling, referrals to healthcare providers, job training, and drug counseling, if needed.

One thing TIP never did while I was there was pass judgment on anyone who engaged in sex work, and instead TIP advocated for legal protections for sex workers, and also provided advice on how to do sex work more safely. Very discreetly, TIP even helped teach individuals how to advertise through the adult services section of Craigslist, as a safer alternative to working the streets or having to go through a pimp. A transgender woman walking the streets, especially if she is black or Latina, is at an extremely high risk for violent hate crimes, and in my six months at TIP I attended a funeral for one of my clients who was killed in a hit-and-run hate crime incident. Police never investigated the crime despite demands from the transgender community.

On November 17, 2011, transgender activists held a demonstration in Washington, DC, at the Metropolitan Police Department Headquarters to protest the failure of police to properly respond to a recent surge in transgender hate crimes. As in Philadelphia, such oversight is hardly surprising at this point. It is merely symptomatic of society's larger failure to recognize how dangerous transphobia—often fueled by religious moralizing—is to individuals. I believe that humanists, atheists, feminists, anti-racist activists, and all those involved in fighting for social justice must recognize their common struggle with the transgender community and speak up when religious leaders help enforce rigid gender roles and sexual taboos that ultimately rob human beings of their inherent dignity.

Groundswell's campaign, even if it has both progressive and conservative religious leaders involved, advances a reactionary moral vision that goes against the best interests of transgender women and sex workers. This moral vision must be opposed. Please tell Groundswell that you want child trafficking stopped—but that their campaign against Backpage-.com is not the way to do it.

CHAPTER 3

Does Globalization Promote Human Trafficking?

Chapter Preface

The term *globalization* refers to the growing trade interaction among countries around the world. This international trade network is enhanced by such factors as free trade agreements and the fact that developed countries have the capital to invest in the cheap foreign labor and production available in developing countries. Although international trade dates back at least to 1295, when Marco Polo returned to Venice with jewels and silk from China, globalization began to be a powerful force after World War II, driven by a variety of factors. Among these factors are free trade, facilitated by accords such as the North American Free Trade Agreement; the rise of capitalism and democracy, driven by the fall of communism and the opening up of China; and technological innovation facilitating global interconnectedness, especially the Internet. As a result, the world today is a much smaller place, with a global marketplace connecting what were once remote places.

In the early decades of the twentieth century, most people worked close to where they were born, got most of their food from local sources, and bought other goods, such as clothing, that were made in their own country. By the late 1900s and early 2000s, globalization made it possible for people to move to regions or countries where there was greater opportunity for work; it also made it feasible for companies in industrialized nations to outsource operations to developing countries where labor is cheaper, and to purchase raw materials or components where they can be most cheaply produced. Globalization at its best has improved per capita income, raised living standards, and facilitated economic and social progress.

Unfortunately, human traffickers thrive on globalization. Unscrupulous businesses keep labor cost low by using workers who are modern-day slaves. Although consumers benefit from cheap items produced through human trafficking, they are unwittingly abetting modern forms of slavery.

In 2011, entrepreneur Justin Dillon with the US Department of State created the website Slavery Footprint, which informs consumers about the sources of the products they buy. Slavery Footprint provides a lifestyle survey that asks consumers about the food they eat; the clothes, toiletries, home furnishings, and electronics they buy; and their hobbies. With this information, the website uses an algorithm to calculate where each item was produced and the conditions under which it was likely produced. Those who eat shrimp may be appalled to learn: "bonded labor is used for much of Southeast Asia's shrimping industry, which supplies more shrimp to the US than any other country. Laborers work up to 20-hour days to peel 40 pounds of shrimp. Those who attempt to escape are under constant threat of violence or sexual assault." Those who wear cotton shirts are faced with these facts: "1.4 million children have been forced to work in Uzbek cotton fields. There are fewer children in the entire New York City public school system." Those who own a smartphone learn that, according to a US Department of State official quoted by the website, "The likelihood that one of these was not touched by a slave is pretty low." Individuals who complete the survey get a score of how many slaves worldwide probably work for them. It is the hope of the website creator that, armed with this knowledge, people will demand products made without slave labor.

Globalization can be a force for good as well as for evil. In the following chapter, selected authors express their opinions on globalization's role in human trafficking.

The Need to Keep Labor Costs Low Leads to the Exploitation of Workers

Siddharth Kara

Siddharth Kara is an affiliate of the Human Rights and Social Movements Program and a fellow at the Carr Center Program on Human Trafficking and Modern-Day Slavery at Harvard Kennedy School of Government.

On New Year's Day 2011, I flew to Lagos to research human trafficking in Nigeria. Towards the end of my trip, I visited a small town called Badagry, about a two-hour drive west of Lagos. In 1502, Portuguese colonists built one of the first slave-trading posts along the coast of West Africa in this city. The non-descript, two-story building still stands today as a museum, but for more than 300 years, it was one of the most active slave-trading outposts in West Africa. Estimates are that almost 600,000 West Africans were shipped from Badagry to the Americas to be agricultural slaves. That figure represents approximately one in twenty of all slaves transported from West Africa to the Americas during the entire time of the North Atlantic Slave Trade.

It was a haunting experience walking through the old slave-holding pens, gazing at the iron shackles, imagining the fear and terror that must have coursed through the veins of slaves as they awaited their fates. Like so many millions today, those 600,000 individuals transported from Badagry to the Americas were victims of human trafficking. In fact, all 12 to 13 million of the West African slaves transported across the Atlantic to the Americas were victims of human trafficking.

While their lengthy journeys at sea are very different from the journeys of most human trafficking victims today, the purpose of those journeys remains the same: the callous exploitation of the labor of vulnerable people in order to maximize profit.

Over the decades, international conventions ... relating to slavery shifted away from targeting actual rights of ownership toward the nature of the exploitation.

The Nature of Slavery Today

However, unlike the agricultural and domestic slaves of the past, today's victims of modern-day slave trading are exploited in countless industries, and they are vastly more profitable. Whether for commercial sex, construction, domestic work, carpet weaving, agriculture, tea and coffee, shrimp, fish, minerals, dimensional stones, gems, or numerous other industries that I have investigated, human trafficking touches almost every sector of the globalized economy in a way it never has before. Understanding the reasons for this shift in the fundamental nature of human trafficking is vital if more effective efforts to combat it are to be deployed. The key thesis to understand is that the slave exploiter's ability to generate immense profits at almost no real risk directly catalyzed the pervasiveness of all forms of contemporary slave labor exploitation.

One point is crucial to establish from the start—slavery still exists. But what exactly is "modern slavery?" There is still considerable debate regarding the definition of terms such as "slavery," "forced labor," "bonded labor," "child labor," and "human trafficking." With "slavery," we can go as far back as the League of Nations Slavery Convention of 1926 and the International Labor Organization's Forced Labor Convention of 1930. These early definitions focused on the exercise of power attaching to a right of ownership over another human being.

Over the decades, international conventions and jurispru-
dence [philosophy of law] relating to slavery shifted away
from targeting actual rights of ownership toward the nature of
the exploitation, particularly as it involves coercion (physical
or other), nominal or no compensation, and the absence of
freedom of employment or movement. The term "forced labor" has generally come to replace the term "slavery," given
the powerful historical and emotional connotations of the lat-
ter term. Similarly, "human trafficking" has come to replace
the term "slave trade."

It is open to debate whether these terminological substitu-
tions are helpful, but when it comes to "human trafficking," I
believe the use of this term has done considerable disservice
to the tactical prioritization required to combat these crimes
more effectively. Definitions of the term "human trafficking,"
such as that found in the United Nations Protocol to Prevent,
Suppress, and Punish Trafficking in Persons (the Palermo Protocol of 2000) or the US Trafficking Victims Protection Act
(TVPA, of the same year), have historically suffered from a
greater focus on the movement connotation of the term "trafficking" rather than the exploitation involved. The result has
been a prioritization of efforts to stop cross-border migration
instead of slave-like exploitation, the real purpose of trafficking; this approach has met with limited success.

---

*Trafficked slaves are moved from countries of origin
through transit countries into destination countries.*

Terminological debates aside, within the broad context of
modern-day slavery, I estimate the number of slaves at the
end of 2010 to have been between 30 and 36 million. Depending on how one specifies terms such as "coercion" and "held
captive," the number of people considered slaves could be
slightly lower or considerably higher. There are many modes

by which slaves are exploited, and these can be aggregated into various categories. I have chosen three: bonded labor, forced labor, and trafficked slaves.

Bonded, Forced Labor, and Trafficked Slaves

The economic model of bonded labor dates back centuries. In essence, individuals borrow money or assets and are bound in servitude until the debts are repaid, and often they never are. Forced laborers are similar to bonded laborers but without the intermingling of credit and labor relationships. However, the line between bonded labor and forced labor is easily blurred. The more farcical a debt becomes, the more the bonded laborer is actually a forced laborer.

Human trafficking is essentially modern-day slave trading, which ensnares millions of people in debt bondage or forced labor conditions in a plethora of industries. Regardless of the industry of exploitation, there are three common steps to the business model of most human trafficking networks: acquisition, movement, and exploitation, which often results in one or more counts of re-trafficking. Acquisition of trafficked slaves primarily occurs in one of five ways: deceit, sale by family, abduction, seduction or romance (with sex trafficking), or recruitment by former slaves. Poor or marginally subsistent individuals are the ones most vulnerable to exploitation because of their economic desperation.

Trafficked slaves are moved from countries of origin through transit countries into destination countries, except in the case of internal trafficking, during which the same country acts as origin, transit, and destination. However, trafficking victims often undergo multiple stops in several countries, where they are repeatedly resold and exploited. At each destination, victims are threatened, abused, and tortured. They may be told they must work off the "debt" of trafficking them between jobs. The accounting of these debts is invariably exploitive, involving deductions for living expenses and exorbitant interest rates. For others, no farce of debt repayment is provided—they are simply kept in a state of perpetual forced labor.

Slave exploiters often re-sell trafficked slaves to new exploiters. If the slaves do not escape, their cycle of exploitation may never end. Even if they do escape, they often return to the same conditions of poverty or vulnerability that led to their initial enslavement, resulting in one or more instances of re-trafficking.

Most importantly, slave exploiters and traffickers take advantage of the fact that movement in the globalized world is exceedingly difficult to disrupt. Borders are porous, documents can be forged, and it can be difficult to identify a potential victim of human trafficking before the forced labor has taken place. Movement is also inexpensive. Whereas ships from Badagry to the Americas had to spend weeks at sea at great expense to transport slaves to the point of exploitation, today's victims of human trafficking can be transported from one side of the planet to the other in a few days or less, at a nominal cost of doing business even when airfare is involved. For these and other reasons, any efforts to combat human trafficking by thwarting movement will prove highly challenging.

In order to truly combat human trafficking, we must understand exactly why it has become so prevalent throughout the global economy.

The final step in the human trafficking business model is exploitation. Exploitation of trafficked slaves primarily involves the coercion of some form of labor or services with little or no compensation. The location and nature of the coercion is industry-specific. In cases of commercial sex, exploitation involves multiple counts of coerced sex acts every day in physical confinement and under threats of harm to the slave or their loved ones back home. The brutality of this form of human trafficking cannot be overstated. It involves rape, torture, forced drug use, and the wholesale destruction of a human body, mind, and spirit.

Another common sector is construction, which may involve exploitation of human trafficking victims under strict confinement at construction sites, with little or no payment for months at a time. In agriculture, trafficked slaves are confined to the area of harvest and are coerced to work under threats of violence or eviction from tenant homes, and with minimal or no wages. When it comes to carpets, trafficked child slaves are locked inside shacks where they are drugged and beaten to work for eighteen hours a day, suffering spinal deformation and respiratory ailments.

The costs of exploiting a slave are miniscule as weighed against the immense profits that criminals can reap.

For these and other products that are tainted by exploitative labor, I have traced the complete supply chains from the point of production to the retailers that sell the tainted products in the United States. This is an important step toward catalyzing the kind of corporate and consumer awareness campaigns required to strike back against the use of trafficked, slave, or child labor in products consumed in Western markets. However, in order to truly combat human trafficking, we must understand exactly why it has become so prevalent throughout the global economy. What compels those involved in this type of exploitation to engage in it?

Incentives Underlying Trafficking

Just like most law-abiding citizens, criminals are rational economic agents, and when a near risk-free opportunity to generate immense profits emerges, they will flock to it. Modern-day slavery is immensely more profitable than past forms of slavery. This is the key factor driving the tremendous demand for new slaves through human trafficking networks. Whereas slaves in 1850 could be purchased for a global weighted average of between US$9,500 and US$11,000 (adjusted for inflation) and generate roughly 15 to 20 percent in annual return on investment, today's slaves sell for a global weighted average of US$420 and can generate 300 to 500 percent or more in annual return on investment, depending on the industry. In terms of risk, the laws against human trafficking and forced labor in most countries involve relatively anemic prison sentences and little or no economic penalties. Even where there are stiff financial penalties stipulated in the law, such as in the United States, the levels of prosecution and conviction of slave exploiters remain paltry.

As a result, the real risk of exploiting trafficked slaves is almost nonexistent. That is to say, the costs of exploiting a slave are miniscule as weighed against the immense profits that criminals can reap. This basic economic reality gives us a clear sense of some of the powerful forces of demand that promote the trafficking and slave-like exploitation of men, women, and children around the world. I believe these forces are also the ones we can most effectively disrupt in the near term.

However, there is also a supply-side to human trafficking, meaning those forces that promote the supply of potential human trafficking victims. We must also mitigate these forces, though it will prove difficult to effect a near-term impact on the human trafficking industry through supply-side efforts alone. The supply of contemporary trafficked slaves is promoted by longstanding factors such as poverty, lawlessness, social instability, military conflict, environmental disaster, corruption, and acute bias against female gender and minority ethnicities.

The policies and governance of economic globalization sharply exacerbated these and other forces during the 1990s. The deepening of rural poverty, the net extraction of wealth and resources from poor economies into richer ones, the evaporation of social safety nets under structural adjustment programs, the overall destabilization of transition economies, and the broad-based erosion of real human freedoms across the developing world all increased the vulnerability of rural, poor, and otherwise disenfranchised populations. These forces unleashed mass-migration trends that shrewd criminals and slave traders could easily exploit. While these global economic and sociocultural supply-side drivers of the contemporary human trafficking industry will require considerable, long-term efforts to redress, we do not have to rely on supply-side measures alone to severely mitigate, if not virtually abolish, human trafficking.

In fact, the demand-side of most human trafficking industries is highly vulnerable to disruption. The specific forces of demand that drive any industry will vary. For example, in commercial sex, male demand to purchase commercial sex is a key factor of demand that would not be present with construction or tea. However, there are always two forces of demand that are common to any human trafficking industry and they are both economic: slave exploiter demand for maximum profit and consumer demand for lower retail prices (the price elasticity of demand).

Human trafficking has evolved from the old world into the globalized world as a key way in which unscrupulous producers can minimize labor costs to advance profits and remain price competitive.

For almost any business in the world, labor is typically the highest cost component to overall operating expenses. Thus, throughout history, producers have tried to find ways to minimize labor costs. Slavery is the extreme of this. Slaves afford a virtually nil cost of labor. With a drastically reduced cost of labor, total operating costs are substantially reduced, allowing the slave owner to maximize profit. However, drastically lower labor costs also allow producers to become more competitive by lowering retail prices. The retail price of any product or service is largely based on the costs of producing, distributing, and marketing that product or service, along with the available supply of the product or alternatives, and whatever brand premium the market will bear. If a major component of cost is stripped out of the production model, then producers can finely balance their desire to maximize profit and lower retail price.

Depending on the product, the lower it costs, the more people will tend to purchase it. Conversely, the more expensive a product is, the less people will tend to purchase it. This concept is called the price elasticity of demand, and depending on the specific product or service, the "elasticity" can be high or low, implying changes in price can have large or small impacts on consumer demand. Because consumers in general almost always prefer the lower priced version of the same product or service (if all other variables such as quality are the same), producers often try to compete by minimizing price, and one of the most effective ways to do this while retaining profitability is to exploit labor.

In a globalized economy, where products are available in our nearby shops from all over the world, the need to be price competitive is greater than ever. A seller of t-shirts or rice no longer just competes with producers nearby, but with producers on the other side of the world. As an example, I was conducting research into bonded labor in South Asia during the summer of 2010, and an exporter of precious stones in Chennai [city in India] told me quite candidly that he was forced to exploit low-wage labor (actually bonded and child labor) in order to compete with the Chinese, who he believed to be doing the same. Because transportation costs are 90 percent less than they were in 1920, and since all types of exploited labor can be used to minimize production expenses, the entire world is in competition, and human trafficking has evolved from the old world into the globalized world as a key way in which unscrupulous producers can minimize labor costs to advance profits and remain price competitive.

Combating Trafficking

Understanding the twin economic forces of demand that have helped catalyze the accretion in levels of human trafficking throughout the global economy suggests two tactical priorities in efforts to combat these crimes. First, attack the profitability human traffickers enjoy. An attack on profitability will reduce aggregate demand for slave labor because slave owners will be forced to accept a lower-profit (hence less desirable) business, or they will pass the increased costs to the consumer by elevating retail price, which will in turn reduce consumer demand.

We are ... far removed from the complex supply chains that may be tainted by trafficked or slave labor at the bottom end of the production process.

The most effective way to attack profitability is to elevate real risk. Depending on the type of industry, the tactics will vary, but such efforts will assuredly involve the following: elevated efforts by law enforcement to proactively investigate and intervene in human trafficking crimes; the expansion of community-based antislavery efforts; elevated funding for anti-trafficking police, prosecutors, and judges, especially in developing nations; fast-track courts to prosecute trafficking crimes quickly so as to minimize risks to the survivor-witness; and a massive increase in the financial penalties associated with human trafficking crimes, including enterprise corruption, asset forfeiture, and victim compensation, to help former slaves get their lives back on track.

An increase in penalties, along with increased prosecution and conviction levels achieved through the kinds of tactics described above, should elevate the real risk and cost of human trafficking to an economically detrimental level. Put in criminal law terms, we are trying to elevate the deterrent and retributive value of the real penalty associated with the commission of slave-related crimes to a far more effective level. In turn, criminals will likely diversify their operations to other, less toxic opportunities, just as quickly as they originally flocked to trafficking and labor exploitation.

The other main force of demand relates to consumers. While we typically prefer to buy our products at the best price, we are also far removed from the complex supply chains that may be tainted by trafficked or slave labor at the bottom end of the production process. However, we are also in control of our consumer force of demand, so it is up to us to demand that lawmakers enact provisions whereby corporations must investigate and certify that their supply chains are free of trafficked, slave, or child labor of any kind. Consumers must also demand that companies whose products they purchase take a leadership role in conducting the kind of investigation and certification required, and that such activities should be a regular aspect of their internal controls and operating model. By attacking the fundamental motivation behind the exploitation of trafficking slaves—profits—and by leveraging consumer power to shift the market away from the "cheap at all costs" product to the product that is morally and socially responsible, a powerful near-term impact can be achieved on the business of human trafficking.

The ugliness of human trafficking dates back centuries, and even though we agreed 150 years ago as a human civilization that slavery is unacceptable, it is more pervasive and expansive today than it was centuries ago when the slave port at Badagry was in its prime. The forces of globalization have made human trafficking a highly profitable and virtually risk-free enterprise. As a matter of ensuring basic human dignity and freedom, the global community must utilize every resource available to combat traffickers and slave exploiters by elevating the real risk and cost of the crime, while eliminating the immense profitability that human traffickers and slave exploiters currently enjoy.

The persistence of human trafficking is an affront to human dignity and a denial of any claims of moral legitimacy by contemporary capitalist civilization. The time is long overdue for the world to come together to deploy the kinds of sustained interventions required to eliminate this evil forever.

Global Recession Boosts Child Prostitution and Trafficking

IRIN: Humanitarian News and Analysis

IRIN: Humanitarian News and Analysis is a service of the United Nations Office for the Coordination of Humanitarian Affairs.

Bangkok, 29 September 2009 (IRIN)Commercial sexual exploitation of children is booming in Southeast Asia, with governments failing to do enough to protect young people, experts say.

"The recent economic downturn is set to drive more vulnerable children and young people to be exploited by the global sex trade," Carmen Madrinan, executive director of End Child Prostitution, Child Pornography and Trafficking of Children for Sexual purposes (ECPAT), said.

"The indifference that sustains the criminality, greed and perverse demands of adults for sex with children and young people needs to end."

According to a recent report by the group, increasing poverty, reduced budgets for social services, and restrictive immigration laws in "destination countries" (which encourage children to avoid detection) are among the factors heightening children's vulnerability.

Added to that, deteriorating household living conditions often compel young people to abandon school to contribute to the family income, exposing them to risk as they seek livelihood options that could result in exploitation, the report states.

The International Labor Organization estimates that sex tourism contributes 2–14 percent of the gross domestic product of Indonesia, Malaysia, the Philippines and Thailand.

According to the UN Children's Fund (UNICEF), an estimated 1.8 million children (mainly girls but also a significant number of boys) enter the multi-billion dollar commercial sex trade annually.

Economic and political pressures

In Thailand, hundreds of factories and projects have closed as a result of the global downturn, leaving thousands of workers—both Thai and foreign—unemployed.

Street children and stateless children are extremely vulnerable to commercial sexual exploitation.

Unemployment is rising at a rate of about 100,000 workers a month and may climb to 1.5 million by the end of the year, specialists say, putting an increasing number of young people at possible risk of exploitation.

"Many people come here and see how cheap it is to buy sex from someone vulnerable, especially in this economic climate, and they delude themselves into thinking they're helping the person out," Giorgio Berardi, programme officer for combating child-sex tourism at ECPAT, said.

Regional dimensions

UNICEF surveys indicate that 30 to 35 percent of all sex workers in the Mekong sub-region of Southeast Asia are between 12 and 17 years old.

Street children and stateless children are extremely vulnerable to commercial sexual exploitation, Amanda Bissex, UNICEF Thailand's chief of child protection, told IRIN.

"We need to improve law enforcement and the economic welfare of children," says Bissex, "but we also need to address people's attitudes and create an environment where there is zero tolerance for abuse of children, whether in their home country or overseas."

Earlier this year, the UN Office on Drugs and Crime (UNODC) stated in its Global Report on Trafficking in Persons 2009 that 79 percent of all global trafficking is for sexual exploitation, one of the world's fastest-growing criminal activities.

The report said the proportion of minors involved in various forms of human trafficking increased from about 15 percent to nearly 22 percent between 2003 and 2007.

In June 2009, the Obama administration expanded the US watch-list of countries suspected of not doing enough to combat human trafficking, putting more than four dozen nations—including Cambodia and the Philippines—on notice that they could face sanctions unless their records improved.

ECPAT also warns that the number of children and young people trafficked within countries is increasing.

Such trafficking frequently involves movement from rural to urban areas or from one city or town to another, without the need for travel documentation. This exploitation is likely to continue proliferating due to the profits generated by sex trafficking.

Globalization Is a Positive Force for Chinese Workers

Erik Kain

Erik Kain is a contributor to Forbes *magazine.*

It turns out that conditions at FoxConn, the Chinese firm that helps manufacture Apple iPads and other devices, are much better than at garment factories and other Chinese factories according to the Fair Labor Association [FLA] which is conducting a review of the plants:

> "Auret van Heerden, president of the FLA offered no immediate conclusions on the working conditions, but he noted that boredom and alienation could have contributed to the stress that led some workers to take their own lives.

> In addition to Foxconn, FLA investigators will later visit facilities of Quanta Computer Inc, Pegatron Corp, Wintek Corp and other suppliers, who are notoriously tight-lipped about their operations.

> After his first visits to Foxconn, van Heerden said, "The facilities are first-class; the physical conditions are way, way above average of the norm."

> He spent the past several days visiting Foxconn plants to prepare for the study.

> "I was very surprised when I walked onto the floor at Foxconn, how tranquil it is compared with a garment factory," he said. "So the problems are not the intensity and burnout and pressure-cooker environment you have in a garment factory. It's more a function of monotony, of boredom, of alienation perhaps."

Boycotting Apple Will Hurt Chinese Workers

Of course, things can always improve, but that's also sort of the point of globalization and expanding markets to developing nations.

Apple makes a good target for anti-globalization rhetoric, I think, even if they're not the most guilty of worker rights violations.

Boycotting Apple and possibly shutting down FoxConn plants in China will not help workers there. Quite the contrary.

The hope of a global economy is that Chinese labor conditions and living standards will improve over time, and that Chinese government will become more open as the economy opens up. This will have a positive, cyclical effect on workers' rights and working conditions throughout China.

This applies to India and the rest of the developing world as well.

One thing that frustrates me when we have this conversation is the assumption that workers in China would somehow be better off without firms like Apple. In the long-run workers in China will be much better off than they are now.

Boycotting Apple and possibly shutting down FoxConn plants in China will not help workers there. Quite the contrary.

I still think it's a basically good thing that people are worried about this, and that groups like the FLA are conducting reviews of working conditions in places like China and India. There are more stories than we can count about abusive conditions at garment factories and elsewhere, not to mention slave labor in some places, and we need to encourage organizations who look out for these things. Sweat shops have been responsible for all sorts of human rights violations, and we need to remain vigilant as consumers.

But overall the introduction of US firms to the Chinese labor market is a good thing for workers there. That so many Chinese workers commit suicide (at higher rates at non-Apple plants, for that matter) tells me that China still has a long ways to go. American firms and the increased prosperity they bring to China will help them create a better society over time.

That's my hope anyways, eternal optimist that I am.

Multinational Companies Can Be a Force for Good

Marc Gunther

Marc Gunther is a senior writer for CNNMoney.com.

Children who are forced to pick cotton in Uzbekistan, farmers scratching out a living in Guatemala and salmon fishermen in Bristol Bay, Alaska, would not seem to have much in common. But all are feeling the global impact of Wal-Mart.

As the world's largest retailer, with $379 billion in revenues last year [2007], Wal-Mart has long been a powerful force in the global economy—a bully, its critics would say. For years, they assailed Wal-Mart for squeezing suppliers over costs, driving mom-and-pop stores out of business or crushing efforts to organize its workers.

Wal-Mart Wants More Ethical Suppliers

These days, though, the company is winning praise for using its leverage—that's a polite term for bullying—to protect the environment and help the poor.

What's changed? Wal-Mart CEO Lee Scott, who announced last month that he will step down in February, has led an ambitious sustainability campaign, opened up to critics and promised to behave more responsibly. One of his last acts as CEO was to convene a summit of Wal-Mart suppliers in China to tell them that they had to adhere to higher ethical and environmental standards.

Consider, as an example, Wal-Mart's confrontation with the authoritarian government of Uzbekistan over child labor.

Last spring, shareholder advocates from pension, labor and investment funds that call themselves socially responsible began a campaign on behalf of Uzbek children who, according to media reports and human rights groups, are forced to pick cotton for low wages and under inhumane conditions. The BBC spotlighted the problem with an eye-opening investigative report that said, among other things, that "for two-and-a-half months a year, classrooms are emptied across this Central Asian nation so that the crop can be harvested."

Uzbekistan is the world's third largest cotton grower and cotton is the nation's biggest export—so pressure from retailers in Europe and the United States could bring about change.

Wal-Mart . . . issued a strong public statement pledging to stop buying Uzbek cotton.

The activist investors, including the nonprofit As You Sow and the Calvert and Domini mutual fund groups, wrote to more than 100 retailers and brands, asking them to trace the cotton used in the goods they sell and avoid Uzbek cotton. Most ignored the letter. (Bed Bath and Beyond, Costco and J.C. Penney were among those who did not respond.)

Others, including Levi Strauss, Target, Limited Group and Gap, agreed to try to exclude Uzbek cotton, according to the shareholder coalition. Wal-Mart went further: It helped organize retail trade associations to pressure the Uzbek authorities and issued a strong public statement pledging to stop buying Uzbek cotton.

"We just thought, this is about as atrocious as it's going to get," Richard Coyle, senior director of international corporate affairs for Wal-Mart, told Fortune. "We just couldn't idly sit by."

As You Sow, an organizer of the shareholder coalition, praised Wal-Mart for its leadership, as did the Interfaith Center on Corporate Responsibility, an alliance of faith-based investors representing more than $100 billion in invested capital.

Because Wal-Mart is asking its suppliers to avoid Uzbek cotton, the company is for the first time requiring them to trace the origins of the cotton they use to make apparel and home furnishings. This is a breakthrough—other retailers had claimed that it was hard or impossible to trace cotton to its source.

"The fact that you have a retailer like Wal-Mart asking for this from suppliers, it's going to have huge ripple effects," said Patricia Jurewicz, associate director of As You Sow's corporate social responsibility program. It means others can be persuaded to follow suit.

Wal-Mart Works with Local Food Producers

In Guatemala, meanwhile, Wal-Mart's stores have begun working with local farmers, in an effort to secure a steady supply of locally grown food while boosting the incomes of some of the poorest people in the region. The company has joined forces with a nonprofit development group called Mercy Corps and with the U.S. Agency for International Development to train about 600 farmers in sustainable agricultural practices, food safety and hygiene, processing and packaging.

"Most of these people are native Mayans, and they've been neglected and marginalized for years," said Karen Scriven, senior director of corporate partnerships for Mercy Corps. "They've never had to grow anything but corn and beans," mostly to feed their families. Now they are selling cash crops desired by Wal-Mart and other retailers including tomatoes, potatoes, yucca and cilantro and other cash crops.

The three-year program will cost $2.2 million—with $600,000 coming from Wal-Mart, $500,000 from Mercy Corps and U.S. AID matching their donations with $1.1 million.

That sounds like a lot of money to train 600 farmers but Scriven says the effort could affect 4,200 family members as well as neighbors.

Wal-Mart agreed to support ... fisheries that are independently certified as sustainably managed.

Manuel Zuniga, vice president of corporate affairs for Wal-Mart Central America, says dealing directly with farmers—thereby cutting out various middlemen—enables Wal-Mart to save money and build relationships with trusted growers who meet its quality standards.

"We can create a loyal base of suppliers who know us well and know what the customer wants," he said. "We can provide a lower price to the customer, as well as a better price to the farmer." You can read more about the project at the Mercy Corps Web site.

Want some fish to go with those veggies? Up in Bristol Bay, Alaska, the world's largest wild sockeye salmon fishery, fishermen are also cheering Wal-Mart because the retailer has agreed to feature their catch as part of its sustainable seafood initiative. They're running newspaper ads in Alaska thanking Wal-Mart for promoting the frozen wild salmon.

Wal-Mart agreed to support the Bristol Bay fishery as part of a commitment made in 2006 that within five years, all of the wild-caught fresh and frozen fish it sells in North America would be sourced from fisheries that are independently certified as sustainably managed. Elsewhere, wild salmon populations have declined from over-fishing.

"This will increase the demand for Bristol Bay salmon, boost fish prices and keep more dollars in Bristol Bay," said Bob Waldrop of the Bristol Bay Regional Seafood Association, an industry group.

To be sure, not everyone is buying into Wal-Mart's sustainability work. The International Labor Rights Forum, an activist group, has an ongoing campaign against Wal-Mart, saying its "ethical sourcing" program is ineffective. Some environmentalists argue that Wal-Mart's business model—selling cheap stuff made all around the world in big-box stores—can never become sustainable.

But they are the dissenters. There's no doubt that Lee Scott has had a profound impact on how Wal-Mart sees its role in the world—and on how the world sees Wal-Mart.

CHAPTER 4

How Can Human Trafficking Be Addressed?

Overview:
The US Government's
Role in the Fight Against
Human Trafficking

US Department of State

The US Department of State is the executive department responsible for the international relations of the United States.

The United States' commitment to fighting modern slavery did not simply materialize 12 years ago with the passage of the Trafficking Victims Protection Act [TVPA] or the adoption the same year of the U.N. Protocol to Prevent, Suppress and Punish Trafficking in Persons, Especially Women and Children (Palermo Protocol). This country's tragic history is not forgotten, nor are the bloodshed and lives lost in the fight to end state-sanctioned slavery.

The Promise of Freedom

The year 2012 will mark the 150th anniversary of the date Abraham Lincoln gave notice of the Emancipation Proclamation. That document and the 13th Amendment to the United States Constitution, following three years later, represent more than policies written on paper. They represent the promise of freedom.

The U.S. Congress subsequently passed laws and federal authorities prosecuted cases in the wake of the Civil War to make clear that this promise of freedom extended to all, from the Hispanic community in the Southwest, to immigrants arriving from Europe, to Chinese workers who built the western railroads, to Native Americans in the Alaska territory.

"The Promise of Freedom," Trafficking in Persons Report, US Department of State, June 2012, pp. 7–31.

A century and a half later, slavery persists in the United States and around the globe, and many victims' stories remain sadly similar to those of the past. It is estimated that as many as 27 million men, women, and children around the world are victims of what is now often described with the umbrella term "human trafficking." The work that remains in combating this crime is the work of fulfilling the promise of freedom—freedom from slavery for those exploited and the freedom for survivors to carry on with their lives. The promise of freedom is not unique to the United States, but has become an international promise through Article 4 of the Universal Declaration of Human Rights and the Palermo Protocol to the Transnational Organized Crime Convention. The challenge facing all who work to end modern slavery is not just that of punishing traffickers and protecting those who are victimized by this crime, but of putting safeguards in place to ensure the freedom of future generations.

A Crime, First and Foremost

A few years ago, stories about human trafficking appearing in the press tended to focus on a victim's suffering or a long-delayed arrest. Those stories still appear. But there is a shift underway. Today, reports on trafficking in persons are about not just the crimes that have been uncovered, but also the many things that people are doing in their communities to eradicate modern slavery. Modern slavery is the centerpiece of new, public-private partnerships and has become a focus for faith-based communities. New developments in supply chain monitoring and corporate social responsibility are producing valuable collaboration between governments and key industries. The modern abolitionist movement is expanding beyond a narrow band of civil society and pockets of concerned government officials. It is entering the public consciousness in a way that builds not just awareness and concern, but also activism and action, both globally and locally. A new generation of informed and interested citizens is beginning to look inward and making the choice to reject lifestyles sustained by exploitation. For all those who continue to live in bondage, this moment could not have come too soon.

As more voices cry out for action to respond to modern slavery, governments must redouble their own efforts and face this challenge head on. . . .

The Victim at the Center

Human trafficking appears in many guises. It might take the form of compelled commercial sexual exploitation, the prostitution of minors, debt bondage, or forced labor. The United States government, and increasingly, the international community, view "trafficking in persons" as the term through which all forms of modern slavery are criminalized.

Why, then, are so many different actions considered the same crime? Why are so many terms used to describe one human rights abuse? Exploitation lies at the core of modern slavery. Whether held on a worksite or trapped in prostitution, a victim of this crime has suffered an infringement of the right to be free from enslavement.

Every single occurrence of modern slavery is happening to a person—someone's sister, mother, brother, father, daughter, or son.

When that right has been compromised, governments are obligated to restore it. The Palermo Protocol's "3P" paradigm of prevention, prosecution, and protection reflects a comprehensive victim-centered approach to ensuring that the rights of individuals are guaranteed. Through prevention measures, governments can work to forestall the violation of rights. Prosecution efforts seek to punish those whose actions have subjugated the lives of their victims through enslavement.

Protection efforts seek to provide appropriate services to the survivors, maximizing their opportunity for a comprehensive recovery.

In this paradigm, strong protection efforts bolster the effectiveness of law enforcement activities and successful prosecutions in turn serve to deter the crime from occurring. A fourth "P"—partnership—is integral to the success of any anti-trafficking strategy. Governments, civil society, the private sector, and the public at large working together will lead to the most effective response to modern slavery.

Like perpetrators of any crime, such as assault or murder, traffickers must be brought to justice. Governments are the only entities that can pass and enforce domestic laws. But just punishing the offender is not enough. Rights that are violated must be restored.

The crime is not abstract; it is about people. Every single occurrence of modern slavery is happening to a person—someone's sister, mother, brother, father, daughter, or son. Protection does not mean only rescue and isolation; although it may require getting someone out of harm's way, protection must be as adaptable and dynamic as trafficking is insidious and unpredictable. Ultimately, true protection means giving victims access to and a choice among options—and recognizing that they are unlikely to choose to participate in shelter and rehabilitation programs that are restrictive or serve merely as pre-deportation waiting periods.

Because this crime undermines the most basic human rights, protection services must be considered just as important as investigating and prosecuting the offenders. The damage inflicted by traffickers can never be undone, but it may be repaired. If governments fail to provide comprehensive protection as a complement to prevention and prosecution efforts, they risk deepening, rather than alleviating, the original harm. . . .

Victims, Survivors, and Providers

Trafficked people have typically been tricked, lied to, threatened, assaulted, raped, or confined. But the term "victim" does not mean that a person who has suffered those crimes was necessarily incapable or helpless. In many cases, these people have shown tremendous strength in the face of horrible adversity.

Sound policy both acknowledges that a crime has occurred and honors victims' agency and autonomy.

People fall victim to trafficking for many reasons. Some may simply be seeking a better life, a promising job, or even an adventure. Others may be poverty-stricken and forced to migrate for work, or they may be marginalized by their society. These vulnerabilities do not mean that those who are victimized are dependent on someone else to empower them. It often means that they had the courage to pursue an opportunity that they believed would change their lives and support their families. Traffickers see and understand this reality, and through imbalances in power and information—and a willingness to use coercion and violence—they take advantage of their victims' hope for a better future.

Law enforcement agents, good Samaritans, and civil society, among others, are often instrumental in helping a victim escape the trafficking situation. For some, though, freedom comes as a result of summoning the courage to escape their abuser when the opportunity presents itself.

Global best practices can serve as useful guides for the effective provision of victim services. These include, for example, the immigration relief given to trafficking victims in Italy; the package of medical, psycho-social counseling, and legal aid provided to suspected trafficking victims in the United Kingdom; or the work authorization given to victims in Taiwan. The specific actions comprising a victim services regime must allow for flexibility to tailor a response specific to individuals' experiences and needs.

Adopting Victim-Friendly Laws and Regulations

The foundation of a government's victim-protection response must necessarily be rooted in that country's anti-trafficking law. An effective anti-trafficking statute provides a clear definition of who constitutes a trafficking victim and sets forth the legal status and recourse to which victims are entitled. This approach flows naturally from the victim-centered, rights-based approach of the modern era; governments should not base their response on nineteenth-century laws that viewed trafficking in persons as the transnational movement of prostituted women, and traffickers as violating state sovereignty by bringing "immoral" persons over the borders. Such an approach is inconsistent with the modern framework established by the Palermo Protocol, which rejected and replaced this outdated formulation with a crime centered on the exploitation of the individual. . . .

Victim Identification

Governments that have put in place victim protection structures cannot idly wait for victims to come forward on their own to seek protection. It is true that some victims escape exploitation through their own courage and determination, but after clearing that hurdle, a victim does not usually know where to turn. He or she is unlikely even to know how to gain access to services from a complex government system, or to have knowledge that a victim referral mechanism exists. Many times, victims do not even know that the abuse they suffered is considered a crime; indeed, they may hide from authorities for fear of punishment, arrest, or deportation.

Traffickers commonly instill such fears in their victims to ensure continued subjugation.

As part of a comprehensive victim protection effort, governments have the responsibility to proactively identify victims and potential victims of trafficking. They have a responsibility to extricate victims from exploitation and, whenever possible, to prevent the crime from occurring in the first place. They have a responsibility to provide victims with the ability not only to leave servitude, but to reenter society as a free man, woman, or child with adequate tools to resume their lives and contribute positively to society.

If governments take proactive measures to look for human trafficking, they will find it.

This is no small task. It requires training, education, and, perhaps most challenging, a change in the way government officials look at vulnerable populations. The first government official a trafficking victim is likely to meet is not a lawmaker or diplomat, but rather a local police officer. If such officers are not trained to identify trafficking victims and understand the nuances of the crime, the victim will likely not be properly identified even if able to articulate his or her story. The services and support described in the pages of a national action plan or an official referral mechanism are irrelevant if the victim cannot first be properly identified and referred to services and protection.

Ultimately, if governments take proactive measures to look for human trafficking, they will find it. It is simply not plausible to claim that, because victims are not self-reporting, trafficking does not occur. . . .

Adaptable, Comprehensive Victim Care

Just as the international norms of protecting victims must be vigorously upheld, the practice of providing victim services must be simultaneously comprehensive and adaptable. Modern slavery takes many forms that require caregivers to provide services reflecting the unique experiences of each survivor. Even if two people endure identical abuse, they may have very different needs.

If shelters are to serve an integral role in a survivor's recovery, they must be places of refuge, not detention centers. Some governments might opt to provide shelter to individual victims in temporary locations, such as rented apartments or hotels, rather than in a central, structured shelter. While that may be the most practical option, governments should recognize that the needs of survivors go well beyond a safe place to stay. They frequently require medical care and counseling, legal advice, and social services—not to mention the means to contact and reunite with their loved ones, if they so desire. Victim care must be designed to anticipate common needs, while responding in a way that is adaptable to each individual's situation.

When victims of trafficking are identified, they often have complex needs that cannot all be met by one person or agency.

To create a victim services model that adequately supports survivors, governments must work proactively to adopt best practices and to develop new and innovative efforts. In countries where a robust civil society plays a key role in advocacy and the provision of services to victims, governments should forge partnerships to benefit from the expertise of nongovernmental organizations (NGOs) and other victim services providers and advocates. Such activity should not be viewed as a way for governments to shift responsibility onto other parties, but instead as an opportunity to forge cooperative arrangements that will take full advantage of the resources and support structures available. Adequate and consistent funding for victim services is a persistent challenge that must be met with a commitment of all involved to work and innovate together.

Additionally, as modern slavery affects a wide range of government concerns, all relevant government agencies should work together to ensure streamlined and effective provision of victim services. If the agencies responsible for immigration, labor, and health care are not communicating, the ability to identify and rescue victims, and to offer efficient and flexible services, will be limited. And if the victim care regime inexorably moves the identified victim toward a preordained outcome of repatriation, the law enforcement mission will suffer as well because victims will be less willing or able to participate in prosecutions of traffickers.

Without the appropriation of adequate resources, a government's approach to victim services can not be sufficiently effective, adaptable, or far-reaching. Around the world, a paucity of funding relative to the scale of the crime hinders those—both within and outside government—who strive to provide services to trafficking survivors. If governments and the international community are serious about making counter-trafficking efforts a priority, it is critical that service providers have the consistent resources and support they need to get the job done.

Law Enforcement—NGO Cooperation

When victims of trafficking are identified, they often have complex needs that cannot all be met by one person or agency. It is necessary that government officials and service providers work together to provide a full range of support, services, and protection. Law enforcement and other government officials should build relationships with NGOs through task forces and community partnerships in order to facilitate this collaboration. For example, if law enforcement officials conduct a raid, NGO partners can be on call to assist with housing support, case management, and medical care. Law enforcement officials and advocates can then work together to provide appropriate safety planning for an individual or group.

The following are areas where a victim may need support:

- Protection from traffickers

- Basic necessities, including food and clothing

- Housing

- Medical and mental health care

- Legal services, including immigration and criminal justice advocacy

- Assistance in accessing public benefits

- Orientation to the local community, public transportation, and other life skills

- Language skills training

- Job training

- Family reunification

Next Steps

Every country is affected by trafficking in persons, and while some countries . . . have met the minimum standards, such an assessment does not mean a government has succeeded in eradicating modern slavery. Indeed, no country is doing enough to end it. As long as the people who survive this crime do not see their traffickers brought to justice and are not able to rebuild their lives, no government will be able to claim complete success in combating modern slavery.

The modern global abolitionist movement is less than a generation old. Success stories have shown us that survivors are eager to overcome their trauma. But too few victims are identified, not enough services are available to survivors, and too few traffickers receive criminal punishment. Many governments around the world have enacted anti-trafficking laws; the next steps in this struggle require governments to implement those laws broadly and effectively. Those who refuse to acknowledge the problem of trafficking are being overtaken by the chorus of governments, businesses, civil society, and men and women around the world who are calling for action and demanding progress in meeting the enormous challenge that remains.

Modern slavery is about people; and the way the world chooses to fight it must also be about people—restoring their hopes, their dreams, and most importantly, their freedom.

The Global Abolition of Human Trafficking

Mark P. Lagon

Mark P. Lagon is ambassador-at-large and director of the Office to Monitor and Combat Trafficking in Persons of the US Department of State.

Human trafficking, whether for forced labor or sexual exploitation, preys upon people on the margins of society and the globalized economy. They include women, children, migrants, and minorities, all treated as less than human. What lessons can be learned on the tenth anniversary of the implementation of both a UN treaty and a comprehensive U.S. law to fight this dehumanizing global crime? What has worked, and what will work best in the future to marginalize human trafficking?

The tenth annual Department of State Trafficking in Persons (TIP) Report estimates that there are 1.8 trafficking victims for every 1000 people in the world.[1] That figure is based on a very conservative International Labor Organization (ILO) estimate of 12.3 million victims globally[2]—less than half of what scholar Kevin Bales estimates.[3] This means that at least one out of every 555 people in today's world is a human trafficking victim.

Ten years ago in Palermo, Italy, UN members finalized an anti-Trafficking in Persons (TIP) protocol to the UN Convention on Transnational Organized Crime.[4] The Palermo Protocol offers a template for fashioning national laws to fight trafficking, and is monitored and supported by the UN Office on Drugs and Crime (UNODC). More valuable than its splashy conferences and awareness emblem underwritten by Persian Gulf potentates, UNODC offers technical assistance to countries to craft laws and has sponsored a handbook for legislators worldwide to do so as well.[5]

In the same year that the Protocol was completed, the United States enacted a sweeping anti-trafficking law, the Trafficking Victims Protection Act (TVPA).[6] It created an anti-TIP Office at the U.S. Department of State to lead diplomatic and interagency endeavors, and to prepare a global report on other countries' efforts. Under the amended TVPA, governments are placed in one of four ranking categories according to legal principles very similar to the UN Palermo Protocol, irrespective of the sheer scale of the problem in a country. Governments are placed on Tier 1 if they are making major efforts and are largely succeeding. They are placed on Tier 2 if they are making significant efforts with mixed results, and on Tier 2 Watch List if they are making some efforts with limited visible impact. Finally, Tier 3 is reserved for governments making negligible efforts. The "Watch List" was added to signal danger of slippage to the Tier 3 category, which also carries potential economic sanctions.

Rule of law consists of much more than laws on the books, whether in the United States or in the least developed of nations.

There remain two major needs to address ten years after the Palermo Protocol and TVPA: realizing rule of law, and helping all groups that are vulnerable to trafficking. An assessment of the last decade and those two needs suggests that the United States is particularly important as the indispensable and chief anti-trafficking voice in the world, and that the business community must step up its own efforts in fighting human trafficking.

The Need for Rule of Law in Practice. Human traffickers treat vulnerable groups such as women, children, migrants, minorities, and disadvantaged castes as if they were not human beings in full. They go unpunished when—through neglect, prejudice, and complicity—societies, businesses, and government personnel permit them to, leaving those vulnerable groups without equal access to justice.

The main tangible impact of the TVPA, U.S. TIP Office's diplomacy, and the Palermo Protocol in the past ten years has been the passage of new laws addressing human trafficking in well over half of the world's countries.[7] This is a major achievement for rule of law and for ensuring equal access to justice for TIP victims.

Yet rule of law consists of much more than laws on the books, whether in the United States or in the least developed of nations. There has been substantial progress in training law enforcement officials and empowering non-governmental organizations (NGOs) to find victims and to provide them access to justice. But transformative change has not yet taken place. Of the three Ps—prosecution of perpetrators, protection of victims, and prevention—which both the Palermo Protocol and TVPA enumerate as areas for state action, prosecution has received the most emphasis to date. The TIP Report documents 7,992 prosecutions in the world in 2003, down to 5,506 in 2009. Of those 5,506, only 432 were for labor trafficking.[8] Prosecutions are limited in general, and minimal for non-sexual exploitation. Implementation of rule of law is lagging, and also deeply needed. Implementation will require more prosecutions to hold perpetrators accountable, and a greater emphasis on victims' access to justice and reempowerment.

The Need to Address All Vulnerable Populations. Human trafficking is very prevalent in a number of areas of the world. South Asia is one of them; of the estimated 27 million TIP victims in the world, some 55 to 75 percent are in India, Pakistan, Bangladesh, and Nepal, chiefly in bonded labor.[9] Another is in China, where the problem takes numerous forms because there are so many vulnerable populations there. Migrating workers move around the country without a safety net. Women are targets of exploitation because of a Wild West sex trade and the female deficit, attributable in great part to sex selection abortion. Uighurs and Tibetans face official discrimination making them vulnerable to trafficking, and North Koreans who flee atrocious political and economic conditions are not rightfully treated as refugees. East Asia is also of particular concern, given the prevalence of human trafficking for both labor and commercial sex. The Gulf is a major flashpoint, where, in spite of some strides prompted by U.S. diplomacy and self-interest, women and foreign guest workers are apt to be treated as lesser humans.

Human trafficking is widespread and takes many forms, but there are not "lesser" victims of this crime. Anti-TIP policy should therefore not privilege some victims over others. Measures taken against TIP have not had wider and more visible effects for a number of reasons, including a "fissuring" of efforts among agencies and countries, and siloed focus on particular vulnerable groups. Anti-TIP policy should not focus on any particular group at the expense of another. For instance, victims of forced labor are no less important than victims of sex trafficking (and vice versa), and sex trafficking is not the only source of exploitation and violence against women.

Some think that sex trafficking has been overemphasized because of alleged moralism, but to focus solely on labor would be equally wrongheaded. It is important that the pendulum not swing toward labor to the near exclusion of adult sex trafficking. The 2010 Report included an informational "box" on "What Is Not Human Trafficking" and emphasizes that prostitution is not trafficking, which is counterproductive.[10] Prostitution is not one and the same as slavery, and few contemporary abolitionists think it is. Still, prostitution enabling environment for sex trafficking, where in brothels, seedy streets, or, until recently, on craigslist.org. Sex trafficking and its basic enabling environment ought not to lose attention.

One sees fissuring of responses elsewhere. Some responses devoted to combating sex trafficking focus only on children. This area is arguably easier for policy responses, given global consensus that there is not meaningful consent by minors to be prostituted. But sex trafficking is not confined to minors. If someone is lured into the sex trade as a minor, does it suddenly become a choice the day someone turns 18? Moreover, numerous adult females in the global sex trade are subject to force, fraud, or coercion—including subtle psychological terror and trickery—which makes them trafficking victims even under the strict standards of the Palermo Protocol.

There is one other serious area of fissuring: "trafficking" may sound like it refers to crossing borders, but it actually refers to turning people into commodities robbed of autonomy. Despite what some at the U.S. Department of Labor, the ILO, and some businesses may believe, crossing borders is not a necessary element of trafficking.

Abolishing human trafficking depends on rule of law and equal dignity, both rightly understood as tests for the efficacy of anti-TIP efforts. Rule of law requires implementation beyond the passage of laws. And the fight for the dignity of human trafficking victims requires equal value and energy accorded to all victims. These two tests will be the basic signs for demonstrating whether the world has successfully embarked on the road toward abolishing modern-day slavery.

There are four important areas of activity that are most important for meeting these two tests of success, and that will be essential to stamping out human trafficking.

American Exemplar. The United States has a moral stake in fighting trafficking; like genocide and HIV/AIDS, such a high-order threat to basic dignity requires the United

States—as the single global power most capable of catalyzing global action—to do so. It also has vital interests in fighting trafficking. It is immensely important to the U.S. economy to sustain the legitimacy of globalization as a largely positive force for broader prosperity. To prove that slavery is not the inexorable product of globalization, and that rule of law can tame globalization's excesses, is an interest, not altruism.

It is worth recalling that Madeleine Albright, the U.S. Secretary of State at the time of the TVPA and Palermo Protocol's promulgation, described the United States as having the role of "indispensable nation" in the world. Despite rancor about the Iraq invasion, legitimacy-sapping treatment of detainees, and economic turbulence, it still remains the indispensable nation. The United States has been the primary anti-trafficking voice in the world for ten years, making a palpable difference by encouraging dozens of nations to address the issue. Yet it could be all the more convincing with the credibility that would come from practicing what it preaches even more.

There has been a clear bipartisan continuity in the TIP Office leadership to increase emphasis on the United States as a good example, using the chairmanship of the inter-agency Senior Policy Operating Group codified by Congress in the TVPA. A central premise of the TIP Office's efforts between 2007 and 2009 was that the United States needed to be an exemplar to be an effective promoter of the anti-trafficking agenda globally. The analogy of how the U.S. Guantanamo, black-site, and enhanced interrogation detainee policies undercut U.S. promotion of freedom, good governance, and credible anti-terrorism policy internationally was obvious at the time.

For example, in the Bush era, the Department of State profiled the United States in the TIP Report, intensively disseminated the Department of Justice (DOJ) annual report on the U.S. record on TIP worldwide,[11] and convinced the DOJ to produce it the same month as the TIP Report (with the "optics" of assessing the United States itself just at the time the United States assessed others). It is tremendous that Secretary of State Clinton has gone further, including a profile with a ranking on lengthier recommendations about areas of weakness in the Report.[12]

The U.S. chapter of the global NGO End Child Prostitution and Trafficking (ECPAT) submitted a comment on the U.S. profile in its report, noting that it did not reflect U.S. Government statistics from 2008 and 2009, which show that almost three times as many prostituted children were arrested as were offered protection and assistance. To be transparent about this very problem of punishing victims, as TIP Officer Director I volunteered to co-lead the U.S. delegation to report to the UN Committee on the Rights of the Child on how the United States was implementing two optional Protocols that it has ratified (on sale and prostitution of children, and on child soldiers).[13] Admitting failings in the areas of the child sexual exploitation protocol was extremely helpful in the United States' constructive leadership role in urging other governments to do more. In the Spring of 2010 at Georgetown University, the South Korean Chairperson of the UN Committee, Yanghee Lee, emphasized the substantial benefit of the U.S. candor.

Concretely, there are three key further steps that the United States should take in order to be a better exemplar. First, the United States should make human trafficking the entrenched focus of domestic policy and spending at the federal, state, and local level, much as domestic violence has become, investing especially in better capacity to give shelter to victims (including prostituted minors). Second, the United States must do what it tells other nations to do: take implementation as seriously as passing laws. The key is to provide law enforcement and prosecutors training, as well as professional incentives to prioritize prosecutions for human trafficking relative to other crimes, given finite resources. Federal officials, Congress, and the fifty State Attorney Generals have it in their power to signal that priority for career advancement. Finally, congressional hearings should examine whether a focus on prosecutions is in effect deprioritizing access to justice for victims. In particular, minors should not be jailed for being prostituted even to encourage testimony against traffickers. Moreover, the United States should adopt the norm of the Council of Europe Convention on Trafficking in Persons that a migrant victim should be given a period to reflect on whether to testify against his or her exploiter, rather than to be further traumatized and face deportation for not cooperating with law enforcement.

A Helping Hand. U.S. efforts to persuade other governments to do more are advanced by offering a helping hand. It is not fully appreciated, but the assistance given to NGOs and more efficacious international organizations like the International Organization of Migration (IOM) is as important a part of the U.S. policy as any. If this fight against human trafficking is about rule of law and access to justice, civil society organizations are crucial partners of law enforcement to identity victims, make them feel safe, and help them. Victims become more stable, helpful witnesses in the process.

A U.S. helping hand can be offered directly to some governments as well. A helping hand does not mean deploying U.S. law enforcement to do the job for or with counterparts in other nations. Above all, it means offering training to other nations' law enforcement branches to help turn law on paper into reality. Law enforcement, immigration officials, and judges worldwide need a helping hand through training to learn to see a victim as a victim, not as a dirty or willful criminal. Governments with a will to change (that is, on Tier 2 and Tier 2 Watch List of the State Department report), but with limited resources, deserve help. Less developed African nations need not so much "grading on a curve" in the U.S. TIP Report (more generous rankings due to lacking governmental capacity) as they need tangible U.S, and multilateral assistance.

Tough Love. Acting as an exemplar and offering a helping hand are important complements to pressuring other governments to increase their anti-TIP efforts. But after ten years of the "tough love" pressure embodied by the TIP Office and its unique report, one that gives grades, is indeed still needed. The TVPA has manifestly worked, as the rankings and global awareness raised by the report has put constructive pressure on govenments worldwide. This has been true even among U.S. allies unused to proddings: Turkey, Israel, the Philippines, the UAE, and even Ireland, which recently appointed an anti-trafficking "czar."

Although some say this "tough love" has not worked, the claim is flatly untrue. The TIP Office and the Report focus the minds of other governments on the problem; and they focus the minds of the U.S. diplomats who would otherwise not have this issue factor into their priorities.

The TVPA Reauthorization Act of 2008, aptly named after British abolitionist parliamentarian William Wilberforce, had one particularly important and welcome provision. It offered a time limit on a country being given a Tier 2 Watch list ranking.[14] This threat of a downgrade should be used, and the waiver authority Congress gave to the Executive Branch to defer or avert an automatic Tier 3 ranking should not be misused in the name of alleged national interests. A so-called "Watch List" is only meaningful if there is a significant prospect of a downgrade to the lowest tier.

As such, Russia and India (7 years at Tier 2 Watch List), and China (6 years) require intensified engagement by the United States and other nations. In all three cases, this engagement will involve going to the top, partners, and sharing lessons with them. First, Presidential and Cabinet-level diplomacy should make clear that human trafficking is not a peripheral U.S. concern relative to economic, counter-terrorism, or nuclear equities. Second, the United States should enlist other great powers in collective dialogue with each of these nations (such as with Russia), for instance at the G-20. Third, the United States should offer examples of what has worked domestically. We must share with India our painful experience of how, in a federal system like its own, U.S. national government action was necessary and possible to make desegregation happen in all states. This too will be the case with bonded labor for disadvantaged castes in India.

There is one other area for tougher love. One of the places where trafficking for labor and victimization of women converge takes place on U.S. soil: domestic servitude for diplomats. A woman from Goa who alleged she was the human trafficking victim of a Kuwaiti official stationed in the U.S. told me something striking in 2008. She said the family treated her far worse as a domestic servant in the United States than in Kuwait because there was even less reason to think they would face consequences in the U.S. than in a Gulf country.[15] That observation should make anyone pause in horror. It was worse in the United States because of the impunity delivered by diplomatic immunity.

It is high time that businesses become more actively and tangibly involved in the global fight against human trafficking.

The U.S. Congress was rightly crystal clear in the TVPA, thrice reauthorized, that attention should be paid to government officials found complicit in human trafficking.[16] Unpunished official complicity is precisely the issue here. It is inevitable that governments may exercise the option to withdraw accused diplomats rather than agree to lift diplomatic immunity to allow U.S. prosecution. Still, to meet the intent of the

TVPA, these cases should be cited in the TIP Report (with using individual names, as has been the case to date with other types of TIP)

The Role of Business. In short, both carrots and sticks, both honey and vinegar, are essential in U.S. diplomacy. Secretary of State Clinton is carrying forward an approach of the Clinton and Bush Administrations to mobilize partnerships with NGOs, philanthropies, and businesses in our foreign policy. She deemed "partnerships" a fourth "P" along with the prosecution of traffickers, protection of victims, and prevention enumerated in the TVPA and Palermo Protocol—more labeling of a continuing, sound, non-partisan policy than introducing an initiative.[17] To be effective, the U.S. Government must go beyond giving money to NGOs and soliciting money from businesses, to coordinating veritable collaborative development of an abolition strategy with these partners.

The business community is a particularly crucial partner. Market demand is a powerful force, and demand for cheap products and commercial sex are drivers of human trafficking. In 2009 the Department of Labor finally fulfilled a 2005 and 2008 Congressional mandate to produce a list of goods tainted by forced and child labor.[18] If consumers knew some businesses were committed to reducing human trafficking, then demand would become an enormous force for good, creating an incentive for businesses to get ahead of the curve and join the fight. Globalization need not inexorably lead to slavery, but it will take the proactive efforts of businesses to prevent it. It is not too much to ask businesses to take preventive action against the most extreme and autonomy-denying forms of exploitation, which are manifestly illegal under international law and most countries' domestic law.

It is high time that businesses become more actively and tangibly involved in the global fight against human trafficking. For ten years, governments, NGOs, and international organizations have dedicated sizeable efforts to fight trafficking.

More definitive results will come, however, if businesses work together to advance an anti-TIP policy. A business coalition would seize the opportunity to leverage varied and unique resources to take a quantum leap in the fight, with the goal of abolishing trafficking. In October 2010, major businesses from sectors as diverse as information technology, soft drinks, cosmetics, labor placement, energy, the auto industry, the airline industry, travel and hospitality, banking, legal publishing, and entertainment met in Washington to explore such a business coalition. A business coalition will be most successful if it goes beyond a single sector (like cocoa or apparel), but nonetheless starts with a modestly sized group of truly committed players attracting others to join.

Businesses should go further than they have to date. They must go beyond merely pursuing dialogue with government and the UN, single-sector accountability efforts, and public awareness efforts not involving accountability of their own business operations. How can human trafficking be abolished if businesses are not fully engaged in working collaboratively across sectors and in reducing enabling environments? If they did so, there would be a much more significant chance to abolish this contemporary form of slavery.

Out of the Shadows. The State Department TIP Office and Report have done much to bring the issue of human trafficking out of the shadows. It is worth thinking about how over the last decade the TIP Office, created ten years ago by the U.S. Congress, has found a formula for exercising public diplomacy more effectively. The TIP Office has told the story of universal values and the partnership the United States offers to extend them. That role has been even more important than the office's traditional diplomacy, and has indeed strengthened that traditional diplomacy.

Maybe that model can help fix the broken U.S. public diplomacy policy. That larger policy has lost its way due to post-Cold War dissolution of the U.S. Information Agency, overreliance on burgeoning private sector television and Internet outlets, ill-conceived ideas that public diplomacy is much like corporate marketing, and occasionally ham-handed forays into engaging the Muslim world after 9/11.

As for human trafficking, bringing the issue out of the shadows is the starting point, and U.S. and multilateral efforts in last ten years have achieved that. Human trafficking victims themselves are indeed in the shadows—socially and economically marginalized groups seen by society and law enforcement as at fault, criminal, or expendable, rather than brutalized and degraded. Human trafficking can slowly but surely itself be marginalized, as slavery was in the 1800s. Among other measures, it will require diplomatic leadership from the U.S. as the enduring "indispensible nation," offering a good example and a helping hand to partners, and strengthened by assistance from the business community. This formula is what it will take to abolish trafficking, so that rule of law is fully realized and that all types victims are offered a chance to reclaim their inherent dignity.

Notes

1. U.S. Department of State, Trafficking in Persons Report 2010, (Washington, D.C., 2010), 7.

2. International labour Organization, "Forced labour," "Internet, www.ilo.org/global/Themes/Forced_Labour/lang--en/index.htm (date accessed: 31 December 2010).

3. Kevin Bales, Disposable People: New Slavery in the Global Economy, 2nd ed. (Berkeley: University of California Press, 2004), 8. An estimate used as the primary benchmark by the major U.S. NGOs is 27 million slaves in the world.

4. United Nations Office on Drugs and Crime, "The Protocol to Prevent, Suppress and Punish Trafficking in Persons, Especially Women and Children, supplementing

the United Nations Convention against Transnational Organized Crime," in the United Nations Convention against Transnational Organized Crime and Protocols Thereto, (New York, 2004), 41–52. For the text of the Protocol and the principal Convention, see www .unodc.org/documents/treaties/UNTOC/ Publications/ TOC Convention/TOCebook-e.pdf.

5. United Nations Office on Drugs and Crime, Combating Trafficking in Persons: A Handbook for Parliamentarians, (New York, 2009). The handbook was developed by UNODC along with the Inter-Parliamentary Union. See www.unodc.org/documents/humantrafficking/UN_ Handbook_engl_cor_low.pdf.

6. Victims of Trafficking and Violence Protection Act of 2000. Pub L No 106–386, 114 Stat. 1464, codified at 22 USC. [section] 7101 (2000 and Supp. 2003, 2005, and 2008).

7. U.S. Department of State, Trafficking in Persons Report 2010, (Washington, D.C., 2010), 45.

8. Ibid.

9. Kevin Bales, Disposable People: New Slavery in the Global Economy, 2nd ed. (Berkeley: University of California Press, 2004), 9.

10. U.S. Department of State, Trafficking in Persons Report 2010, Washington, D.C., 2010), 8.

11. See, for instance, U.S. Department of Justice, Attorney General's Annual Report to Congress and Assessment of U.S. Government Activities to Combat Trafficking in Persons Fiscal Year 2008.

12. U.S. Department of State, Trafficking in Persons Report 2010, (Washington, D.C., 2010), 338–345.

13. U.S. Department of State, "Initial Report Concerning the Optional Protocol on the Sale of Children, Child Prostitution and Child Pornography," Internet, www.state.gov/g/drl/rls/84467.htm (date accessed: 31 December 2010).

14. William Wilberforce Trafficking Victims Protection Re-authorization Act of 2008. Public L No 110–457, 122 Stat. 5044, codified at 22 USC. [section] 7101 (2008), sec 107(a).

15. See the treatment by the American Civil Liberties Union of Tina Fernandez in the case of Sabbithi, et al. v. Al Saleh, et al., Internet, www.aclu.org/humanrights -womens-rights/case-prifile-sabbithi-et-alv-al-saleh-etal (date accessed: 31 December 2010).

16. Victims of Trafficking and Violence Protection Act of 2000, sec. 108(b)(7).

17. Hillary Rodham Clinton, "Partnering Against Trafficking," The Washington Post (17 June 2009).

18. U.S. Department of Labor, Bureau of Labor Affairs, The Department of Labor's List of Goods Produced by Child Labor or Forced labor, Internet, www.dol.gov/ ilab/programs/ocft/PDF/2009TVPRA.pdf (date accessed: 31 December 2010).

The Trafficking Victims Protection Act Needs to Be More Supportive of Child Victims

Bridgette Carr

Bridgette Carr is a clinical assistant professor and director of the Human Trafficking Clinic at the University of Michigan Law School.

Human traffickers prey on the vulnerabilities of other people. Poverty, lack of education, and language barriers are keys that human traffickers use to successfully exploit others. For foreign national children who have been trafficked in the United States, these same vulnerabilities are often ignored by the immigration system.

From its inception, the Trafficking Victims Protection Act (TVPA) has been touted as a tool to combat grave human rights violations that affect children. In fact, the TVPA's legislative history is rife with stories, statistics, and anecdotes involving children—often young girls.

The TVPA has always recognized the failure of a one-size-fits-all approach for victims of trafficking, and that the needs of child victims can be quite different than the needs of adult victims. In light of this reality, a number of TVPA provisions make special exceptions or accommodations for children. On paper, these accommodations may seem satisfactory. Unfortunately, for trafficked children within the immigration system, like the ones described below, the reality can be quite different.

Bridgette Carr, *Examining the Reality of Foreign National Child Victims of Human Trafficking in the United States*, 37 Wash. U. J. L. & Policy 183 (2011), http://digitalcommons.law.wustl.edu/wujlp/vol37/iss1/8 Copyright © 2011 by the Washington University Journal of Law and Policy. All rights reserved. Reproduced by permission.

The Child Victim

Jacqueline was born in a small town in West Africa. She loved going to school and dreamed of getting a good education. Her trafficker took advantage of her dream. When Jacqueline was thirteen, her trafficker convinced Jacqueline's parents that she could receive an education in the United States. The trafficker promised to provide Jacqueline with an education and a quality of life in the United States comparable to the level that the trafficker provided to her own daughter. Jacqueline was sad to leave her family but excited about the educational opportunities awaiting her in America. Jacqueline was fourteen when she arrived in the United States. Unfortunately, her education was in the form of enslavement. Jacqueline was forced to work twelve to sixteen hours a day, she had to hand over all of her money to her traffickers, and she was never allowed to go to school.

Because Jacqueline was classified as a child victim of human trafficking, she had access to a number of social services and legal benefits.

Jacqueline was rescued almost two years after she arrived in the United States. Immediately after her rescue she lied about her identity and age when questioned by law enforcement. She was still afraid of her traffickers and worried about what would happen to her and her family if she told the truth. Eventually she told law enforcement agents about her life working against her will for the trafficker. Fortunately, the agents believed her.

Jacqueline's encounter with law enforcement—in her case, Immigration and Customs Enforcement (ICE)—is one of, if not the most, pivotal points in her case. If the agents had not believed her story or if they had identified her as a noncitizen living in the United States without permission rather than as a victim of human trafficking, all the benefits built into the TVPA for children would be irrelevant because she would not have access to them.

But because Jacqueline was classified as a child victim of human trafficking, she had access to a number of social services and legal benefits. She was provided with housing, a caseworker, medical care, and therapeutic services, Jacqueline also had access to an attorney. For the first time since she arrived in the United States, she was enrolled in school.

But being rescued was only the first step. Jacqueline had a variety of legal needs: her traffickers were being prosecuted in federal court; she wanted to apply for a trafficking visa (T visa); and she wanted to be reunited with her family.

Victimized as a Child, Rescued as an Adult

Sally, like Jacqueline, was a young girl in West Africa. She too dreamed of attending school in the United States. Sally and Jacqueline were both trafficked by the same traffickers. In fact, the girls even lived under the same roof at times, but Sally was not at the apartment when the ICE agents rescued Jacqueline.

Long before Jacqueline was rescued, Sally had publicly challenged the trafficker and threatened to call for help. The trafficker responded swiftly with physical violence and sent Sally back to West Africa. The trafficker shamed Sally within her home community and then forced Sally to teach girls—recruited by the trafficker—the hair braiding trade so that the recruits would immediately be ready to work when they arrived in the United States. Sally was devastated and tried to tell members of her family the truth about the traffickers. But only one family member believed her and helped her escape.

Sally's escape route brought her back to the United States. She was unable to remain in her home country because the trafficker was powerful there and Sally had already been ostracized and shamed due to the trafficker's lies. To return, Sally had to use the fraudulent visa that the trafficker had forced her to use during her initial entry into the United States. This time, however, she had to live the life connected to that visa. This meant that Sally, a fifteen-year-old from West Africa, would now be forced to live as the wife of a thirty-five-year-old man in the United States.

After the ICE agents rescued Jacqueline they learned about Sally and quickly found and rescued her. When Sally was rescued, she was eighteen years old and had spent the previous three years being forced to support her "husband" and bear his children. After four-and-a-half years, Sally was finally free.

Like Jacqueline, Sally had a variety of legal needs: her traffickers were being prosecuted in federal court; she wanted to apply for a T visa; she needed a valid work authorization to support her children; she wished to reunite with her mother; and she wanted her real name on her children's birth certificates.

Exploited but Denied Recognition as a Victim

Jacqueline was not the only child in the apartment on the morning the ICE agents entered. There were other girls who, like Jacqueline, were classified as victims by the ICE agents. In addition to the girls inside the apartment, there was also a five or six year old little boy, Miles. Like Jacqueline and Sally, Miles was brought to the United States under a fraudulent visa. Unlike the girls who admitted that they were forced to work for the traffickers, Miles denied that he worked for the traffickers. Based on this answer, the agents determined that Miles was not a victim of human trafficking.

Thus, Miles was considered a noncitizen living in the United States without permission. As such, Miles was served with a Notice to Appear in removal (deportation) proceedings. In addition to being charged with being in the United States without permission, Miles was also charged with procuring his own admission or visa to the United States by "fraud or by willfully misrepresenting a material fact." Miles, an infant when he received his visa, was nevertheless charged with using fraud or willful misrepresentation to obtain the visa. The ICE agent who served Miles with the Notice to Appear was, ironically, also the victim witness specialist for the local ICE office.

While Jacqueline and the other girls were provided with services under the TVPA including safe housing, caseworkers, therapists, and lawyers, Miles was sent to an immigration detention center for children. Miles had a variety of legal needs, not least of which was fighting his deportation.

Children who have been victims of a severe form of human trafficking . . . are eligible for a T Visa.

The stories of Jacqueline, Sally, and Miles offer a unique opportunity to evaluate the TVPA in practice. All three children were brought into the United States under fraudulent visas procured by the same traffickers. All three lived together in an apartment owned by the same traffickers. All three worked, in some capacity, for the traffickers in their shops. Though the facts are similar, the impact of the law is not.

Jacqueline

As a foreign national victim of a severe form of human trafficking, Jacqueline could request an eligibility letter from the Department of Health and Human Services. This letter qualifies foreign national child victims for a wide array of benefits.

As an unaccompanied foreign national child victim of human trafficking, Jacqueline qualified for and was accepted into the Unaccompanied Refugee Minor (URM) Program. The URM Program includes specialized resettlement and foster care services for unaccompanied refugee minors and eligible child victims of human trafficking. Children who enter the

United States prior to age eighteen can remain in foster care/ independent living until they complete high school or reach twenty or twenty-one years of age. . . .

Because Jacqueline was a child victim of a "severe form of human trafficking" she was also eligible to apply for a T Visa. Children who have been victims of a severe form of human trafficking, are physically present in the United States on account of human trafficking, who would face extreme hardship involving unusual and severe harm if removed, and who meet certain immigration requirements are eligible for a T Visa. A T Visa gives trafficking victims the right to live and work in the United States for four years. A T Visa applicant may also bring certain family members to the United States. The sooner of three years from the date of receipt of the T Visa or completion of the prosecution or investigation into the trafficking incident, a T Visa holder may apply for legal permanent residence. . . .

A lot has changed in Jacqueline's life in the almost three years since she submitted her T Visa application and the derivative applications for her parents and siblings. The traffickers have either pled guilty or been convicted. All of them have been sentenced. Jacqueline was awarded her T Visa and is now enrolled in school full time. Though Jacqueline submitted the necessary information about her family members when she applied for her T Visa, her family still remains in Africa. . . .

Unfortunately one huge obstacle remained before [her family] could reunite with Jacqueline: money. The total cost for Jacqueline's family to come to the United States including the passport fees, DS-160 application, and airline tickets was almost $10,000. This represents an almost insurmountable fee for Jacqueline and her family as the average yearly family income in Jacqueline's country is approximately $400 according to UNICEF's 2008 country report. The bitter irony is that Jacqueline earned more than enough money while working under the traffickers to pay these costs.

Sally

After Sally was rescued she was placed in the same URM Program as Jacqueline. Though Jacqueline thrived in the URM Program's foster care placement, it was extremely difficult for Sally because she had previously supported her household, including two of her own children. Before her rescue, she was responsible for making all of the money and taking care of her children. Placing Sally in an environment where she was viewed as a child was a difficult adjustment. Sally did not fit the paradigm of a child victim because her enslavement had taken away her childhood. Unfortunately, the placement options within the URM Program did not recognize and serve Sally's complex reality.

Like Jacqueline, Sally received continued presence status soon after her rescue. Continued presence only lasts for one year and must be renewed by law enforcement. As an adult Sally could not immediately apply for her T Visa, she was eighteen when she was rescued and therefore was required to show that she cooperated with all reasonable requests of law enforcement in order to apply. The ICE agents working on Sally's case refused to provide the certification of her cooperation until the prosecution and sentencing of Sally's traffickers was completed. For Sally, this meant waiting over two years before she could even apply for a T Visa. As a result Sally's continued presence had to be renewed multiple times. During this two-year period the ICE agents failed to timely renew Sally's continued presence and Sally accrued unlawful presence. It was not until 2010 that Sally received the law enforcement certification of her cooperation and was finally able to apply for her T Visa.

Still, Sally needed more legal assistance. For three years, Sally had lived a life in the United States under someone else's name. She bore children under that name, held a job, and paid taxes. One of her first requests to the Clinic was to change the mother's name on her children's birth certificates. It upset

Sally that the mother's name on both certificates was an identity foisted on her by her trafficker and used against her by her "husband." The Clinic is currently working to fix these birth certificates. Additionally, Sally hopes to reunite with her family. Due to the delay in obtaining her T Visa, it is unclear how long it will take for Sally's family to obtain derivative visas and enter the United States.

Miles

Classifying Miles as a noncitizen living in the United States without permission meant that he would not be viewed as a victim of human trafficking and would not receive the same benefits as Jacqueline and Sally. As such, Miles was separated from the people he knew to be his family and sent to an immigration detention facility. Miles was put in federal custody and was ineligible for the URM Program; instead, he was placed into the Division of Unaccompanied Children's Services (DUCS) program. Children in DUCS can be placed in a variety of settings, from detention centers to foster care placements and Miles was eventually moved into foster care after his initial placement in a detention facility.

Miles was now eligible for adoption, two-and-a-half years after he was found in the home of the traffickers.

Miles struggled in foster care. As a child in a DUCS foster care placement, he did not have access to the same level of support services as Jacqueline and Sally in the URM program. Yet he desperately needed those services. He had never been to school nor had he interacted much with children his age or adults in the outside world. The person he identified as his mother had been taken away by the "police," and the girls he identified as his sisters went to foster homes. In addition to therapy, Miles' caseworker told Clinic students that he needed stability and permanency in his foster care placement. Neither of those goals could be accomplished until his immigration case was resolved because he was not eligible for adoption while in removal proceedings. . . .

After a multitude of twists and turns, and with the support and assistance of an understanding family court judge, the Clinic was able to obtain Special Immigrant Juvenile Status (SIJS) for Miles. With the granting of SIJS, Miles was no longer in removal proceedings. Unfortunately, his identity, parentage, and country of origin were still unknown and this presented unique problems before he was eventually granted legal permanent resident status.

All individuals who are trafficked as children should be eligible to apply for a T Visa regardless of whether they cooperate with law enforcement.

With his immigration issues resolved, Miles was now eligible for adoption, two-and-a-half years after he was found in the home of the traffickers. This did not have to happen to Miles. Had there been a chance to reconsider his status as a victim once the full facts of his experience were known, I have no doubt that the ICE agents would have considered Miles a victim of human trafficking. However in that critical moment when he was discovered in the trafficker's home, the ICE agents decided he was a noncitizen living in the United States without permission, a noncitizen who, as an infant, attempted to defraud the U.S. government. This decision meant that Miles spent the next two-and-a-half years fighting to stay safe in the United States, rather than healing from the abuse he had suffered.

Making the TVPA Supportive of Child Victims

The plights of Jacqueline, Sally, and Miles highlight a number of areas where the TVPA must be improved. First, the "snapshot moment" must be lengthened. The critical determination of whether a child is a victim of human trafficking or a noncitizen living in the United States without permission should not be left to a law enforcement agent in the heat of a rescue or raid. Ideally, a young child, like Miles, found in a home where all of the other minors were classified as victims of human trafficking, should be presumed to be a victim of human trafficking. In Miles' case the presumption seemed to be the opposite and the burden was on Miles to prove otherwise. Requiring a young child to provide the evidence necessary to prove that he was a victim of human trafficking immediately following a raid by armed law enforcement agents is unfair and unrealistic. Absent a presumption in favor of classifying such a child as a victim of human trafficking, the child should be provided access to an attorney before the decision is made. At a minimum, victim witness specialists who are trained to interview traumatized children should interview all children who might be victims of trafficking. The Department of Homeland Security should have trained child forensic interview specialists conduct these interviews.

All individuals who are trafficked as children should be eligible to apply for a T Visa regardless of whether they cooperate with law enforcement. Currently, individuals who are under eighteen years of age at the time of the filing of their T Visa application are exempt from the requirement to provide evidence of cooperation with law enforcement. This exemption should be extended to all individuals who were trafficked as children. Limiting the exemption to individuals who are rescued from their trafficker's control and who manage to file the T Visa before turning eighteen is an artificial distinction. All individuals who were trafficked as children need the ability to file the T Visa without a certificate of cooperation from with law enforcement. Individuals who were trafficked as children but who are unable to file until they are adults should not have their status, their ability to work, and their ability to reunite with family members delayed because of a lack of co-operation with law enforcement or law enforcement's decision to wait for the termination of a prosecution or investigation before providing certification.

Amendments must be made to the TVPA to prioritize family reunification. The bureaucratic hoops and prohibitive costs that currently stand in the way of this goal should be eliminated. The traffickers kept Jacqueline away from her family for two years and the process of trying to bring her family into the United States has kept them separated even longer; almost three years at the writing of this article. And now, the costs associated with Jacqueline's family members' trip to the United States may result in Jacqueline being separated from her family indefinitely. Family members who are at risk of retaliation by the traffickers can be paroled into the United States and this provision should be revised to allow all individuals trafficked as children to reunite quickly with their family members.

At a minimum, once the underlying T Visa has been approved and the relationship between the derivative and the child victims has been established, family members should be admitted pending a biometrics check upon their arrival in the United States. Requiring family members to navigate fingerprint cards and background checks for months on end before granting them an opportunity to reunite with their children is unreasonable when alternatives are feasible. One such alternative would be for the family members to go through an in-person interview at the closest U.S. Embassy at which time a biometric exam could be conducted. The interview could be conducted prior to the family members' flight out of the origin country and the biometrics check would provide adequate protection from identity fraud.

Finally, the cost of airfare should not be the ultimate barrier preventing child victims of human trafficking from reuniting with family. The United States must support the funding of programs like IOM's anti-trafficking projects to assist victims of trafficking, and reunite family members with victims like Jacqueline and Sally. But the IOM program is not enough. Funding must be provided to all child victims of human trafficking who want to reunite with their family members. Without this funding, the ability to bring family members into the United States under the TVPA is an empty promise for many victims, especially children.

The goals of the TVPA, to protect and support child victims of human trafficking, can be realized by understanding the TVPA's failures in real cases. The TVPA must be amended to allow for more careful classification of whether a child is a victim. The TVPA must provide trafficked children with the opportunity to apply for a T Visa without making it contingent on cooperating with law enforcement. More importantly, the TVPA must provide a timely and realistic route for child victims to reunite with family. Without these amendments the TVPA will continue to fail foreign national children who have been trafficked in the United States.

Stopping Human Trafficking Requires a Grassroots Effort

Ruth Dearnley and Steve Chalke

Ruth Dearnley is chief executive officer of Stop the Traffik, a global movement fighting human trafficking through community involvement. Steve Chalke is a special advisor to the United Nations on Community Action against Human Trafficking.

How much would you pay for a winter coat? How much would you pay for the child that made it?

Slavery Exists Today

Fifty years ago, the abomination of slavery seemed like a thing of the past. But history has a way of repeating itself. Today, we find that human slavery is once again a sickening reality. At this moment, men, women and children are being trafficked and exploited all over the world: 2.4 million have been trafficked into forced labour worldwide. Of these, 600,000 to 800,000 are trafficked across borders each year and 12,000 children are working as slaves on cocoa plantations in West Africa. It is impossible to ever reach a consensus on the true scale of the problem but, regardless of the figures, what matters is that human trafficking is big and getting bigger. What matters is that every number represents a human life destroyed. It is happening on every continent and in almost every country: whether the place we live is a source, destination or transit point for trafficking, none of us can claim to be wholly unaffected by this crime.

As the extent of human trafficking is recognized, a number of approaches to tackling it have been developed. Stop the Traffik is one such approach. Born out of witnessing first-hand the effects of human trafficking, we started out in 2006 as an informal coalition dedicated to raising awareness of trafficking and generating the political will necessary to stop it.

International trafficking will inevitably raise issues of immigration, but its victims cannot simply be treated as illegal migrants.

During our short existence we have found that one of the biggest impediments to anti-trafficking efforts is a lack of understanding of the issue. Trafficking, and consequently, the measures taken to combat it, is often entangled with people smuggling, immigration and asylum, prostitution and other forms of organized crime. It must be emphasized that the essence of trafficking is the forced exploitation of individuals by those in the position to exert power over them. While moving people is an intrinsic part of trafficking, this may occur within as well as across borders, and it may take a variety of forms. If they have been tricked or deceived, a person may even willingly transport themselves into a situation of exploitation. But unlike those who pay to be smuggled into another country, victims of trafficking have no prospect of making a new life for themselves.

International trafficking will inevitably raise issues of immigration, but its victims cannot simply be treated as illegal migrants, nor can the efforts to tackle it be reduced to stricter border controls. We can find sex trafficking abhorrent without taking a particular stance against prostitution, and policies to reduce or control the sex industry are just one approach to ending the trade of human flesh. Finally, despite the similarities between the organized trafficking of drugs, arms and humans, which may require comparable police tactics to combat, we commit a grave injustice against the victims of human slavery if we reduce them in our minds to the status of commodities.

Human Trafficking Is a Complex Crime

The first step to preventing human trafficking and prosecuting the traffickers is therefore to recognize the complexity of the crime which cannot be tackled in a vacuum. Anti-trafficking strategies have to be embedded in every policy area, from improving female education in source countries so that girls are less vulnerable to trafficking, to increasing police pay in destination countries so that officers are less susceptible to bribery. We cannot allow ourselves to marginalize the issue of trafficking, viewing it as something that can be ended with a few extra taskforces or dedicated units. We need everyone to be aware of how it affects them, and what they can do to stop it. Laudable efforts in this direction have already been made. In 2000, the United Nations launched the Protocol to Prevent, Suppress and Punish Trafficking in Persons, which established a victim-centred approach to trafficking. It has since been signed by 177 countries. In 2005, the Council of Europe Convention on Action against Trafficking in Human Beings marked a step towards greater cooperation and dedication within Europe.

But more needs to be done. Many people still do not know what trafficking is, or do not care. We are working to change that, at every level of society. In February 2008 we delivered 1.5 million signatures to the UN from people calling for an end to human trafficking; as a result, our founder Steve Chalke was appointed UN.GIFT Special Advisor on Community Action against Human Trafficking. Since then we have continued to build on our grassroots support, firm in the belief that trafficking cannot be stopped by international conventions alone. Our focus is currently geared towards three key campaigns.

Three Campaigns Fight Trafficking

First is Start Freedom, our dynamic new global project run in conjunction with the UN that aims to engage and raise awareness among young people, helping them learn about the issues surrounding human trafficking. The fact that over half of all victims of human trafficking are under 18 empowers young people to realize the importance of their potential to prevent this illicit trade. Already we've had stories from source, transit and destination countries such as Greece, Mexico and Nepal, about how young people, schools, faith groups, and communities are engaging with Start Freedom. Communities are at the heart of our campaigns. During Freedom Week in March 2010, young people will connect, engage and share in their communities' varied and creative ways to mark their objection to human trafficking.

Only with a concerted effort by governments, private companies, non-governmental organizations, and above all communities, can we hope to end the horror of human trafficking.

Our other key project at the moment is Active Communities against Trafficking (ACT), which aims to bring together members of a community under the umbrella of an ACT group. We equip these groups with an abundance of resources to help them identify trafficking, understand how it affects local communities, and learn how to help prevent its continuation. They can do this by asking questions about missing children and by forming connections with local authorities, professionals and community leaders. We believe trafficking starts in a community, and can be stopped by a community, and as the ACT project takes hold across countries, we are witnessing the profile of trafficking being raised, bringing together a diversity of people to help combat human trafficking in its various guises. The second stage of ACT, currently being piloted, will be launched in 2010. It is essentially a community research project that aims to gather information about human trafficking for sexual exploitation in local communities. This project has strong potential to contribute immensely to our key objectives: prevention of trafficking, prosecution of traffickers and protection of victims.

A third central focus is our Chocolate Campaign, which is informed by the fact that more than a third of the world's cocoa comes from Côte d'Ivoire, where child trafficking and forced labour has been widely documented and acknowledged by international initiatives, such as the International Cocoa Initiative. Since international deadlines for eradicating child trafficking were missed by manufacturers, we decided to campaign ourselves by trying to get the big chocolate manufacturers to tell us that their products are "traffik free". Up until very recently, most of them could not guarantee this—quite simply because their supply chains were not free of child slavery. Our Chocolate Campaign encourages people to help spread awareness about child trafficking in the cocoa industry, and to pressurize big chocolate manufacturers to commit to certifications, such as Fair Trade or Rainforest Alliance, which are currently the best guarantees we have to indicate that products are "traffik free". Our campaign strategy relies on our numerous grassroots supporters: people host Fair Trade Chocolate Fondue fundraisers, send letters and make phone calls to manufacturers, boycott brands until they become Fair Trade, and hold awareness-raising events to inform and empower others to make ethical decisions. Our successes so far have been fantastic: Cadbury committed to a Fair Trade Dairy Milk, and Mars promised to certify the Galaxy bar with the Rainforest Alliance by 2010, and their whole range by 2020. Within a few weeks of targeting Nestlé to commit to a fair trade Kit Kat, we got news that they too were following suit in the United Kingdom by introducing a Fairtrade four-finger Kit Kat in January. This is a start, but it is nowhere near the end.

Only with a concerted effort by governments, private companies, non-governmental organizations, and above all communities, can we hope to end the horror of human trafficking. Stop the Traffik has developed into an independent charity with over 1,500 member organizations and hundreds of thousands of individuals around the world who refuse to tolerate the existence of slavery in the twenty-first century.

People are talking, communities are rising, global networks are being forged and governments are responding to the united message that human trafficking must end.

Stricter Laws and More Vigorous Prosecution Are Needed to Combat Sex Trafficking

Chuck Neubauer

Chuck Neubauer is a staff writer for The Washington Times.

When she first showed up at Children of the Night, a privately funded residential facility, "Jane" was angry. Arrested more than 20 times as a prostitute, she had been hardened by the street. She threw things at her counselors. Everyone was terrified by having to deal with her.

"She was just afraid. She was used to being treated so rough," said Lois Lee, the Los Angeles group's founder and president. "She didn't know what to do with someone nice."

Jane, not her real name, was just 14 when her life was taken over in Seattle by a 36-year-old man who said he loved her and promised to give her a better life. It was an easy sell: She was the product of a troubled home, where she was sexually molested by her father's roommate. The abuse began when she was 4 years old. She also was molested at the day care center where she was taken every day.

"My mom was a junkie," Jane, now 17, said in an interview. "I lived with my dad. He was up and down with his moods. He had a marijuana addiction. . . . I can't remember much of my childhood. I block it out."

Jane said the molestation made her shy, and when she finally told someone about it—her aunt—her father turned away from her. "I needed his support, but he started to shut down," she said. "I figured he didn't care anymore [about me] and so I didn't care anymore. I just started staying away from my house."

She ended up with a family friend, a woman who forced her to work as a prostitute and sell drugs. That's when she met James Jackson, the man she called Jay, who persuaded her to go with him to Portland. Ore. He promised to show her a better life, but moments after they arrived, Jackson told her she had to "sell her ass," court records show. When she objected, he choked and punched her until she agreed to be a prostitute.

Analysts say the number of children sexually exploited in the U.S. or at risk of being exploited is between 100,000 and 300,000.

Jane is not the only girl to fall victim to someone she has trusted, but no one really knows how many others there are.

Sex trafficking is so widespread, said Nathan Wilson, founder of the Project Meridian Foundation in Arlington, which helps police identify traffickers and their victims, that "no country, no race, no religion, no class and no child is immune." He said 1.6 million children younger than 18—native and foreign-born—have been caught up in this country's sex trade.

But, he said, the number of victims is hard to quantify because of the lengths to which traffickers go to keep their crimes hidden.

Analysts say the number of children sexually exploited in the U.S. or at risk of being exploited is between 100,000 and 300,000.

"We know it is a really large number," said Anne Milgram, a former high-ranking federal prosecutor who tried and oversaw sex trafficking cases. "We know there are a lot of children being victimized. We just can't tell you what number."

Never-Ending Stream

Rachel Lloyd said she has seen a "never-ending stream" of abused girls since she founded Girls Educational and Mentoring Services (GEMS) in New York City in 1997, which helps girls and women ages 12 to 24 victimized by sex traffickers.

"We don't know the number, but we know it is happening. I am working with 300 girls now," she said, adding that most came from troubled homes where there was either sexual or physical abuse. "For every single woman I have met that was exploited, you could tell why they ran away and why they were easy prey for a pimp. The pimp becomes their strongest connection in life."

With an estimated annual revenue of $32 billion . . . human trafficking is tied with arms dealing as the world's second-largest criminal enterprise, behind only drugs.

Ms. Lloyd speaks from experience: Sexually abused as a child in England, she ended up in Germany and at 17 was working in a strip club, where she met an American she thought loved her but who "pimped me out." She said he beat her to keep her working and when she finally escaped, she was "broken emotionally and physically" before putting her life back together.

The Washington, D.C.-based Polaris Project, which advocates stronger trafficking laws and provides help to victims, has said trafficking for sex and forced labor generates billions of dollars in profits by victimizing millions of people globally. It said the average age of entry into the sex trafficking industry in the U.S. is between 12 and 14 years old.

With an estimated annual revenue of $32 billion, or about $87 million a day, law enforcement authorities, government agencies and others say human trafficking is tied with arms dealing as the world's second-largest criminal enterprise, behind only drugs. U.S. Immigration and Customs Enforcement (ICE), the lead agency in trafficking investigations, has estimated that 800,000 people are trafficked into sex and forced-labor situations throughout the world every year.

U.S. Attorney Rod Rosenstein in Maryland said the sex trafficking of minors is a top priority of his office, but bringing offenders to justice has become more difficult in recent years. He said the traffickers' use of the Internet has made it harder to locate their victims, meaning that many of the girls and young women are no longer on the street or at truck stops where law enforcement can see them.

Mr. Rosenstein helped create the Maryland Human Trafficking Task Force in 2007, which—working with state, federal and local law enforcement authorities, along with private agencies—seeks to rescue trafficking victims and prosecute offenders.

Since its creation, the task force has sent many traffickers to prison, including Lloyd Mack Royal III, 29, of Gaithersburg, who received a 37-year sentence in July [2010] for using what prosecutors said was "physical violence, drugs, guns and lies" to force three girls younger than 18 into prostitution. A federal judge also ordered that after his release, Royal must register as a sex offender.

Kiss His Pinky Ring

According to court records, Royal forced the girls to engage in sex; threatened to harm them and their families; hit the girls and held one of them at gunpoint; gave them cocaine, PCP, marijuana and alcohol before forcing them to have sex with customers; and, to assert his authority, forced them to "kiss his pinky ring." The records show he drove the girls to hotels in Gaithersburg and the District to engage in sex.

Royal also gave the girls drugs before forcing them to engage in sex with him to test their "sexual aptitude," according to the records.

Last month [March 2011], Derwin S. Smith, 42, of Glen Burnie, Md., pleaded guilty in a task force case to transporting a 12-year-old D.C. girl to Atlantic City, N.J., to work as a prostitute. She was rescued by the task force after she called a relative.

Maryland task force members Amanda Walker-Rodriguez and Rodney Hill, Baltimore County prosecutors, said in an FBI law enforcement bulletin in March that 300,000 American children are at risk of becoming victims of sex traffickers. They said the children often are forced to travel far from home and their lives revolve around "violence, forced drug use and constant threats." They called sex trafficking in the U.S. a "problem of epidemic proportion."

"These women and young girls are sold to traffickers, locked up in rooms or brothels for weeks or months, drugged, terrorized, and raped repeatedly," they said. "The captives are so afraid and intimidated that they rarely speak out against their traffickers, even when faced with an opportunity to escape."

A guy from the neighborhood recognized her and rescued her.

For many law enforcement officers, the crime can be deeply personal.

"When I heard what happened, I cried," said Sgt. Chris Burchell, a 28-year veteran of the Bexar County, Texas, Sheriff's Office when he learned that a 13-year-old girl had been kidnapped, raped and forced to work as a prostitute in a San Antonio crack house. He has since founded a nonprofit group called Texas Anti-Trafficking in Persons, which builds rapid-response coalitions across the state.

In the San Antonio case, Juan Moreno, 45, was convicted in December and sentenced to four life terms. Prosecutors said he charged crack customers $25 to rape the teenage girl, who had come into the house with a friend looking for drugs and was held for more than a week.

"He threatened to kill her," said Kirsta Melton, an assistant Bexar County district attorney who prosecuted the case. "She was literally tied to the bed. . . . A guy from the neighborhood recognized her and rescued her." She said the neighbor had refused an offer of sex and "figured out a way to get her out."

"It never occurred to me how many child sex trafficking cases there were," said Ms. Melton, now in charge of such prosecutions for the county.

Knows Firsthand

Ms. Milgram, the former New Jersey attorney general, also knows firsthand about prosecuting trafficking cases. She tried two of the Justice Department's biggest international sex trafficking cases and one of the first ever under the federal Trafficking Victims Protection Act of 2000. In that case, two sisters went to prison for 17 years for forcing Mexican girls, some as young as 14, into prostitution. Later, she became the lead prosecutor for sex trafficking cases.

Now teaching a course in human trafficking law at New York University, Ms. Milgram said prosecutors need to bring more cases. The 243 her Justice Department office brought between 2000 and 2009, she said, were "a great start but not enough." She also said local prosecutors were not getting the job done and that while New York City advocacy groups have identified hundreds of sex trafficking victims, New York police have made only a small number of arrests.

"We have to do better," she said.

The issue of sex trafficking has attracted the attention of several elected officials. This month [April 2011], Oregon passed a bill establishing harsher penalties for sex trafficking, as did Texas. Maryland passed three such bills this month to pay for training in schools, to give law enforcement additional surveillance and wiretapping tools, and to remove prostitution convictions from sex trafficking victims' records.

Similar laws were enacted this month in Minnesota, Nevada, Missouri, Tennessee, New York and Michigan.

State Sen. Renee Unterman, a Republican from Gwinnett County, outside Atlanta, has been pushing for years to strengthen Georgia's sex trafficking laws. She said it has been "very, very tough" to get men to talk about the issue, but added that people are starting to understand that the girls should not be treated as criminals but as victims. She said more services and facilities are needed to treat them, but it is "very costly to take care of these types of victims."

Georgia lawmakers passed a bill last month [March 2011] that toughens penalties for people who traffic children for sex. The bill is awaiting the governor's signature.

On one occasion when . . . she had not made enough money, she said, he pushed her down and punched her in the face.

Made to Feel Subhuman

Jane's fall into the world of sex trafficking began in May 2008, just before her 15th birthday. Jackson, her pimp, forced her to work as a prostitute in Portland. When she protested, he beat her. "He made me believe I was not human and I was just for one thing—to make money for him," she said, calling her life a nightmare and suffering bruises and scars from many beatings.

Asked why she didn't leave, she said, "I had nowhere to go. I didn't know anybody. Where was I to go? He threatened to kill me all the time."

On one occasion when he got mad because she had not made enough money, she said, he pushed her down and punched her in the face, saying, "You are going to die tonight." She said she pleaded for her life and promised to do whatever he said: "Just don't kill me. I thought I was going to die."

Of that beating, the FBI later said, "She awoke to find Jackson holding a firearm at her head and swearing on his mother's life that he would kill her." The bureau said that "several times a week," Jackson choked her, pulled her hair, pushed her and struck her with his hands, a belt and a coffee pot, and that he "tried to bite off her finger."

"I trusted him even after all this stuff. After he abused me, I still thought it was love—I thought that this is how it was supposed to be. . . . Most of our arguments were about money," she said, adding that she had sex with six men a day, sometimes eight or nine. "I was bringing him $600 a day, but he wanted more."

Jane got out of that life when she was arrested in October 2008 and an FBI agent asked her whether she wanted to go to Children of the Night, where she now lives. She said it was the first time she was treated like a victim instead of a criminal. "I had the FBI on my side. I could actually tell they were trying to help me," she said.

She since has earned her high school diploma, and is attending college and getting help at a place where, she said, "people actually care about me."

But the memories persist: "It still affects me . . . in a very, very scary way. I am scared when I walk out the door to walk to the bus to go to school. In class, I am scared to raise my hand. I am scared someone is going to hurt me. I am scared to sit in the front row because there are too many people behind me I can't see."

Jackson pleaded guilty in March. Sentencing is scheduled for June 3 [2011] in Portland, where he faces a minimum of 15 years in prison. In announcing the plea, U.S. Attorney Dwight C. Holton in Oregon said: "Human slavery is alive and well—as cases like this make all too clear. We have got to put an end to this violent trade in young women and girls."

Organizations to Contact

The editors have compiled the following list of organizations concerned with the issues debated in this book. The descriptions are derived from materials provided by the organizations. All have publications or information available for interested readers. The list was compiled on the date of publication of the present volume; names, addresses, phone and fax numbers, and e-mail and Internet addresses may change. Be aware that many organizations take several weeks or longer to respond to inquiries, so allow as much time as possible.

Amnesty International
5 Penn Plaza, 14th Floor, New York, NY   10001
(212) 807-8400 • fax: (212) 463-9193
e-mail: aimember@aiusa.org
website: www.amnestyusa.org

Amnesty International is a nongovernmental organization that campaigns for internationally recognized human rights. By providing articles, pamphlets, and video media, Amnesty International seeks to educate people about human rights violations and call people to action. The organization publishes regular reports about worldwide human trafficking, including "Human Trafficking at the US Southwest Border" and "The Worst Place to Be a Woman in the G20."

Anti-Slavery International
Thomas Clarkson House, The Stableyard
Broomgrove Rd., London   SW9 9TL
   UK
44 (0)20 7501 8920 • fax: 44 (0)20 7738 4110
e-mail: info@antislavery.org
website: www.antislavery.org

Anti-Slavery International, founded in 1839, is the world's oldest international human rights organization and the only charity in the United Kingdom that works exclusively against slavery and related abuses. Along with partner organizations around the world, Anti-Slavery International focuses on debt bondage, forced labor, forced marriage, child slavery, human trafficking, and descent-based slavery. In addition to an extensive library of publications available on its website, the organization publishes the quarterly magazine, *Reporter.*

Coalition Against Trafficking in Women (CATW)
PO Box 7427, Jaf Station, New York, NY   10116
fax: (212) 643-9896
e-mail: info@catwinternational.org
website: www.catwinternational.org

The Coalition Against Trafficking in Women (CATW) is a nongovernmental organization that promotes women's human rights by working internationally to combat sexual exploitation. Founded in 1988, CATW was the first international nongovernmental organization to focus on human trafficking, especially sex trafficking of women and girls. CATW's website contains information about trafficking in women all over the world, including articles, reports, resolutions, speeches, and statements.

Coalition to Abolish Slavery and Trafficking (CAST)
5042 Wilshire Blvd., No. 586, Los Angeles, CA   90036
(213) 365-1906 • fax: (213) 365-5257
e-mail: info@castla.org
website: www.castla.org

The Coalition to Abolish Slavery and Trafficking (CAST), a nonprofit organization, was established in 1998 in the wake of the El Monte sweatshop case regarding seventy-two Thai garment workers who were kept for eight years in slavery and debt bondage. CAST was created to provide intensive case management, comprehensive services, and advocacy to survivors healing from the violence endured during slavery. The CAST website provides links to a variety of resources, including reports, issue papers, training guides, and legal resources.

End Child Prostitution, Child Pornography and Trafficking of Children for Sexual Purposes (ECPAT International)

328 Phayathai Rd., Ratchathewi, Bangkok   10400
   Thailand
+662 215 3388 • fax: +662 215 8272
e-mail: info@ecpat.net
website: www.ecpat.net

ECPAT International is a global network of organizations and individuals working together for the elimination of child prostitution, child pornography, and trafficking of children for sexual purposes. It seeks to encourage the world community to ensure that children everywhere enjoy their fundamental rights free and secure from all forms of commercial sexual exploitation. In addition to an annual report, ECPAT publishes a number of resources, including "Commercial Sexual Exploitation of Children: FAQs" and "Combating Child Sex Tourism: FAQs."

Free the Slaves

1320 19th St. NW, Suite 600, Washington, DC   20036
(202) 775-7480 • fax: (202) 775-7485
e-mail: info@freetheslaves.net
website: www.freetheslaves.net

Free the Slaves is a nonprofit, nongovernmental organization that campaigns against slavery and human trafficking. Free the Slaves was formed in response to Kevin Bales's book, *Disposable People*, which brought readers' attention to modern-day slavery. The organization's website provides links to videos, books, research, and articles on human trafficking, including "Recommendations for Fighting Human Trafficking in the United States and Abroad" and "Ending Slavery: How We Free Today's Slaves."

Global Rights

1200 18th St. NW, Suite 602, Washington, DC   20036
(202) 822-4600 • fax: (202) 822-4606

e-mail: info@globalrights.org
website: www.globalrights.org

Global Rights is a human rights advocacy group that partners with local activists to challenge injustice by promoting women's human rights and combating discrimination on the basis of race, ethnicity, or sexual orientation. With offices in countries around the world, Global Rights helps local activists create just societies through proven strategies for effecting change. Global Rights maintains an extensive collection of resources regarding human trafficking, including "Combating Human Trafficking in the Americas: A Guide to International Advocacy" and "Human Rights Standards for the Treatment of Trafficked Persons."

Human Rights Watch
350 5th Ave., 34th Floor, New York, NY   10118-3299
(212) 290-4700 • fax: (212) 736-1300
e-mail: hrwnyc@hrw.org
website: www.hrw.org

Human Rights Watch is a nonprofit, nongovernmental human rights organization that conducts research and advocacy to combat human trafficking. Each year Human Rights Watch publishes more than one hundred reports and briefings on human rights conditions in some eighty countries, including "Sex Workers at Risk" and "If You Come Back, We Will Kill You."

HumanTrafficking.org
1825 Connecticut Ave., Washington, DC   20009
fax: (212) 884-8405
website: http://humantrafficking.org

The HumanTrafficking.org website is a project of the Center for Gender Equality of the Academy for Educational Development. The purpose of the website is to bring government and nongovernment organizations in East Asia and the Pacific together to cooperate with and learn from each other in an effort to combat human trafficking. The website provides country-specific information such as national laws and action plans and descriptions of anti-trafficking activities worldwide. HumanTrafficking.org maintains an extensive library of publications on the subject of the sale and trade of humans.

Shared Hope International
PO Box 65337, Vancouver, WA   98665
(866) 437-5433
e-mail: savelives@sharedhope.org
website: www.sharedhope.org

Shared Hope International is a nonprofit organization with the Christian mission of rescuing and restoring women and children in crisis through education and public awareness. Shared Hope International partners with local groups to help women and children enslaved in the sex trade by providing them with shelter, health care, education, and vocational training opportunities. In addition to an extensive library of interviews and press releases, Shared Hope International also publishes books, including *From Congress to the Brothel: A Journey of Hope, Healing, and Restoration.*

Stop the Traffik
75 Westminster Bridge Rd., London   SE1 7HS
   UK
+44 (0)207 921 4258
e-mail: info@stopthetraffik.org
website: www.stopthetraffik.org

Stop the Traffik is a global movement consisting of individuals, communities, and organizations fighting to prevent human trafficking around the world. The organization works to inspire, inform, equip, and mobilise communities to know what human trafficking is, know how to protect themselves and others, and know how to respond. Stop the Traffik's website includes a wealth of information to help individuals and communities develop and implement local campaigns to educate leaders and stop trafficking in their region. These materials include videos, training aids, flyers, fundraising kits, and other publications.

World Health Organization (WHO)

Avenue Appia 20, Geneva 27   1211
   Switzerland
+41 22 791 21 11 • fax: +41 22 791 31 11
e-mail: info@who.int
website: www.who.int

The World Health Organization (WHO) is the directing and coordinating authority for health within the United Nations system. It provides leadership on global health matters, shapes the health research agenda, sets norms and standards, articulates evidence-based policy options, provides technical support to countries, and monitors and assesses health trends. Several of its many investigative reports have focused on human trafficking, including "Trafficking of Women and Children for Sexual Exploitation in the Americas."

Bibliography

Books

Kevin Bales — *Disposable People: New Slavery in the Global Economy*, rev. ed. Berkeley: University of California Press, 2004.

Kevin Bales and Ron Soodalter — *The Slave Next Door: Human Trafficking and Slavery in America Today*. Berkeley: University of California Press, 2009.

Alison Brysk and Austin Choi-Fitzpatrick, eds. — *From Human Trafficking to Human Rights: Reframing Contemporary Slavery*. Philadelphia: University of Pennsylvania Press, 2012.

Anthony M. DeStefano — *The War on Human Trafficking: U.S. Policy Assessed*. Piscataway, NJ: Rutgers University Press, 2007.

Anne T. Gallagher — *The International Law of Human Trafficking*. Cambridge, UK: Cambridge University Press, 2010.

Hille Haker, Lisa Sowle Cahill, and Elaine Wainwright, eds. — *Human Trafficking*. London: SCM Press, 2011.

Anna Jonsson — *Human Trafficking and Human Security*. London: Routledge, 2009.

Siddharth Kara — *Sex Trafficking: Inside the Business of Modern Slavery*. New York: Columbia University Press, 2009.

Min Liu
Migration, Prostitution, and Human Trafficking: The Voice of Chinese Women. New Brunswick, NJ: Transaction, 2011.

Harold J. Newton, ed.
Human Trafficking: Scope and Response Efforts. New York: Nova Science, 2012.

Shiro Okubo and Louise Shelley, eds.
Human Security, Transnational Crime and Human Trafficking: Asian and Western Perspectives. New York: Routledge, 2011.

Joel Quirk
The Anti-Slavery Project: From the Slave Trade to Human Trafficking. Philadelphia: University of Pennsylvania Press, 2011.

Louise Shelley
Human Trafficking: A Global Perspective. Cambridge, UK: Cambridge University Press, 2010.

Julian Sher
Somebody's Daughter: The Hidden Story of America's Prostituted Children and the Battle to Save Them. Chicago: Chicago Review Press, 2011.

Daniel Walker
God in a Brothel: An Undercover Journey into Sex Trafficking and Rescue. Downers Grove, IL: InterVarsity Press, 2011.

John Winterdyk, Benjamin Perrin, and Philip Reichel, eds.
Human Trafficking: Exploring the International Nature, Concerns, and Complexities. Boca Raton, FL: CRC Press, 2012.

Gillian Wylie and Penelope McRedmond, eds. *Human Trafficking in Europe.* Houndmills, UK: Palgrave Macmillan, 2010.

Periodicals and Internet Sources

Tresa Baldas "Human Trafficking a Growing Crime in the U.S.," *Detroit Free Press*, January 22, 2012.

Jeff Ballinger "How Civil Society Can Help: Sweatshop Workers as Globalization's Consequence," *Harvard International Review*, Vol. 33, No. 2, Summer 2011.

Alison Bass "Why Shutting Down Backpage Won't Eliminate Sex Trafficking or Underage Prostitution," *Huffington Post*, June 29, 2012. www.huffington post.com.

Martin Cizmar, Ellis Conklin, and Kristen Hinman "Real Men Get Their Facts Straight: Ashton and Demi and Sex Trafficking," *Village Voice*, June 29, 2011.

Charles Duhigg and David Barboza "In China, Human Costs Are Built into an iPad," *New York Times*, January 25, 2012.

Daniel Fisher "Backpage Takes Heat, but Prostitution Ads Are Everywhere," *Forbes*, January 26, 2012.

Marc Gunther "The Bigger Picture Behind Apple's China Problem," GreenBiz.com, February 7, 2012. www.greenbiz .com/blog.

Helen Hu
"The Dark Side of Globalization: Whether Lured in, Kidnapped, or Sold by Their Families, Modern Slavery Represents a Big, Old Problem in a New, Smaller World," *Diverse Issues in Higher Education*, Vol. 28, No. 7, May 12, 2011.

Roy Huijsmans and Simon Baker
"Child Trafficking: 'Worst Form' of Child Labour, or Worst Approach to Young Migrants?" *Development & Change*, Vol. 43, No. 4, July 2012.

Nicholas D. Kristof
"She Has a Pimp's Name Etched on Her," *New York Times*, May 23, 2012.

Mark P. Lagon
"How to Stop Human Trafficking," *The American*, January 16, 2009. www.american.com/archive.

Nick Pinto
"Women's Funding Network Sex Trafficking Study Is Junk Science," *Village Voice*, March 23, 2011.

Julie Ruvolo
"Sex, Lies, and Suicide: What's Wrong with the War on Sex Trafficking?" *Forbes*, June 26, 2012.

Amanda Walker-Rodriguez and Rodney Hill
"Human Sex Trafficking," *FBI Law Enforcement Bulletin*, Vol. 80, No. 3, March 2011.

Steven Watt
"Trafficking in War Zones: Making Zero-Tolerance Meaningful," American Civil Liberties Union, April 30, 2012. www.aclu.org/blog.

Women News   "STOP Google Adwords from
Network   Internet Sex-Trafficking of Women
                and Girls," Change.org, February 23,
                2012. www.change.org.

Women News   "U.S. Congress Questions Google
Network   About Sex-Trafficking," Trustlaw.com,
                April 24, 2012. www.trust.org
                /trustlaw.

Index

O

Obama, Barack (administration), 84
Oppressed groups, 34

P

Pakistan, 107–108
Palermo Protocol
    adoption of, 94–95
    paradigm of prevention, 96
    US role and, 110
    victim assistance with, 99, 105–107
Petriliggieri, Francesca, 23–29
Philippines, 16, 83, 84
Polaris Project, 34, 140
Poverty, and human trafficking
    alleviation programs for, 20–21
    as cause, 23–29
    education need, 27–29
    gender role and, 26–27
    migration role and, 24–25
    as only one cause, 30–32
    risks from, 23–26
Prevention programs for human trafficking, 20–22
Price elasticity of demand, 78
Profitability issues, 79–81
Project Meridian Foundation, 139
Prostitutes Education Network, 64
Prostitution
    of children, 19, 82–84, 144–146
    economic and political pressures, 83
    as human trafficking, 15, 108–109
    online advertisements for, 44–47
    overview, 82–83

regional dimensions, 83–84
restricting online classified advertising, 48–56
slavery vs., 108
visibility issues in advocacy, 52

R

Race and ethnicity concerns, 33–35
Rai, Rupa, 27
Rainforest Alliance certifications, 136
Rape concerns
    of children, 19, 45, 142
    in human trafficking, 22, 75, 98
Recruitment techniques by human traffickers, 26
Rosenstein, Rod, 141
Royal, Lloyd Mack, III, 141
Runaways, 34, 62
Ruppen, Erich, 28
Russia, 113

S

Safe-sex supplies, 65
Schapiro Group, 40
Scott, Lee, 88, 92
Scriven, Karen, 90–91
Senior Policy Operating Group, 110
Sex-power industry, 54–56
Sexual exploitation/sex trafficking
    as human trafficking, 15, 23, 133
    marketplace for, 38
    online, 37–40
    overview, 138–139
    prosecution for, 138–146

163

CPSIA information can be obtained
at www.ICGtesting.com
Printed in the USA
FFOW05n0836240813
1654FF

[2]